Alethea Ballard

maverick
QUILTS

Using Large-Scale Prints,
Novelty Fabrics & Panels with Panache

C&T PUBLISHING

Text copyright © 2011 by Alethea Ballard

Photography and artwork copyright © 2010 by C&T Publishing, Inc.

Publisher: Amy Marson

Creative Director: Gailen Runge

Acquisitions Editor: Susanne Woods

Editor: Liz Aneloski

Technical Editors: Nanette S. Zeller and Gailen Runge

Copyeditor/Proofreader: Wordfirm Inc.

Cover/Book Designer: Kerry Graham

Production Coordinator: Jenny Leicester

Production Editor: Julia Cianci

Illustrator: Aliza Shalit

Photography by Christina Carty-Francis and Diane Pedersen
of C&T Publishing, Inc., unless otherwise noted

Published by C&T Publishing, Inc., P.O. Box 1456, Lafayette, CA 94549

Library of Congress Cataloging-in-Publication Data

Ballard, Alethea, 1964-

 Maverick quilts : using large-scale prints, novelty fabrics & panels with
panache / Alethea Ballard.

   p. cm.

 ISBN 978-1-60705-232-6 (softcover)

 1. Quilting--Patterns. 2. Appliqué--Patterns. I. Title.

 TT835.B26375 2011

 746.46--dc22

                          2010040914

Printed in China

10 9 8 7 6 5 4 3 2 1

contents

Dedication and
Acknowledgments . . . 4

Introduction 5

Use That Fabric 6

   Choose Those Fabrics 6

   Use These Fabrics Too . . . 7

   Alter That Fabric 9

   Selective Cutting 11

   Raw-Edge Appliqué 13

Sew That Fabric:
Quilting Basics 14

   Fabric Requirements 14

   Seam Allowances and Sewing 14

   Making Friends with the Feed Dogs . . 15

   Lacing the Blocks Together 16

   Cutting 17

   Pressing 17

   Pinning 18

   Borders 18

   Backing 20

   Batting 20

   Layering 20

   Basting 20

   Quilting 20

   Binding 21

Projects 23

   Fly By   23

   Show Off   27

   California Housetop   31

   Square Dinkum   36

   Bella Boxes   41

   Superstars   45

   Jalousie   54

   Goddess   60

   Dishes   65

   Lovely Landscape   73

About the Author . . .79

Dedication

To the ladies and gents at my fabric stores:

The Cotton Patch, especially Linda, Heidi,
Tina, Jocelyn, and Carolie

The former Quilter's Inn, now Wooden Gate Quilts,
especially Jane, Marby, Margaret, Pat, Joni, and Cyndy

Thimblecreek, especially Sue, Laurie, Chickie,
Roxie, and Joe

Stone Mountain and Daughter, where the crew
barely bats an eyelash when I put 30 bolts of fabric
on the cutting counter!

Dan at The Sewing Machine Shop

You guys keep me going and keep me "using that fabric."

Acknowledgments

I want to thank my family and friends for their
support and encouragement in making this book.
I love you guys.

I am also very grateful to my nieces and nephews for
all the love and kindness they give me. Stewart, Megan,
Caitlin, Marley, Hannah, Harley, David, John, Stephen,
Lucia, Eli, Olivia, and Danny: I am a lucky auntie!

Millions of thanks to the thousands of students
I have had at Stanley Middle School; you guys rock!

Thank you to Liz Aneloski, Nanette S. Zeller,
Kerry Graham, and my wonderful editors at C&T.

Thanks to Michael Miller Fabrics for their fabric
contributions.

Hugs and kisses to my wonderful husband, Steve.

And my most special thanks go to my personal trainer,
Mac Dodds; you have taught me so much about being
positive, and you have been there every step of the
way, encouraging, understanding, and supporting me.
Stupendous!

introduction

What is this talk about fabric, and what is this baloney about the Maverick Quilter? Well, here goes:

Once upon a time, a little girl named Alethea made a quilt, and she fell in love with fabric. For many years her mother dragged her to fabric stores, and she always wanted to get some of everything. For her tenth birthday all she wanted in the world was a sewing machine. She made her first quilt that year and continued to sew as she grew up. After many disastrous attempts at skirts and a glorious pair of high-waisted, suspender-clad, pink-and-white-striped, cropped 80s pants, she realized that squares were much easier, and that was pretty much it.

My journey as a quilter is like many others: sew a quilt, make mistakes, have successes, and learn and get better. I always loved drawing quilt designs on graph paper, coloring them in, and then getting the fabrics to make the quilt. This worked pretty well for a while.

Then one day I just turned a corner, and instead of choosing a quilt design and buying fabric to go with it, I started buying fabric first (*Geisha Landscape*, page 78). I would look at it and decide how much of the fabric I wanted to see in the quilt, what size I wanted those pieces to be, and I would begin to cut. Gathering fabrics to go with the featured fabrics came next, and sewing pieces, cutting, playing, altering, exploring—eventually it all came together, and a quilt was born. This creative, spontaneous working style really lets me enjoy being a quilter. I don't feel constrained by rules, shoulds, and shouldn'ts. There is no finger wagging in my sewing room.

Of course, I have to be open to the possibility of mistakes, but they have usually turned to out to be happy accidents, and some of the best parts of my quilts have been created that way.

The Maverick Quilter was born out of this working style. A maverick is a person who doesn't do things the way everyone else does and is okay with that. I break the rules. I sew odd fabrics together, I sew crookedly, I buy fabric without a plan in mind, and I have even given quilts away without attaching a label! Ooo!

There is a maverick inside all of us, and I encourage you to tap into that little quilt rebel inside of you to play, explore, and create with joy.

You can use this book in several ways. You can read all about my process and begin to create your own personal style and creative voice. You can use it for the techniques and tips provided to make you a more well-rounded quilter. Or you can use it for the individual quilt project instructions provided—or a combination of all three. And be sure to read all the great tips, notes, and "Maverick Quilter Says" sprinkled throughout the book.

I am thrilled to have you join me on this fabric-lover's journey.

use that fabric

Choose Those Fabrics

Okay, so I'm at the fabric store buying nice matchy-matchy fabrics for a conservative, yet pleasing, project, and I come across a bolt of bold, colorful novelty print fabric that I absolutely love. I pick it up. I caress it, tenderly tracing the patterns. Then I put it under my arm and start carrying it around. I just can't part with it. I'm thinking, "What on earth would I do with this—it's too precious. I can't cut it up, I don't need another piece of fabric, my stash is too big already!" But I can't seem to put it down, and when I get to the cutting table, I sheepishly ask for a little. "Just a half a yard…Better make it one…You know, I think I'll need two," I stammer to the lady cutting for me. "I have no idea what I am going to do with this," I blurt out, blushing. But I buy it and bring it home, and, ignoring the project I am supposed to be working on, I look at it lovingly for days.

Over the years, this happened to me many times—and perhaps it happens to you too. The question was, "What am I going to do with it?" I couldn't stand the idea of cutting it up, for fear that I'd "lose it forever," yet I couldn't think of the perfect project. So I'd wait and wait. Six months later, when I was cleaning up my sewing room, I'd find it buried under something and sigh as I added it to the stack of novelty prints in my crowded stash. So often these fun prints didn't seem to go into any quilt design I'd seen. The charm or whimsy of the print could be lost in the cutting. And the intimidation factor kept me from using these gems.

It took me a long time to actually start using these fabrics in quilts, because I was always afraid to "waste" any if the quilt turned out to be a flop. Finally I just started cutting up the fabrics and using them. I haven't wrecked one yet, nor have I looked back.

While each of my projects is very different, there is method in my madness. The size and scale of the print usually directs me to develop a way to show it off. Once I decide the best way to showcase the fabric, I just jump in and start making blocks. Each element is added as the project takes shape on my design wall, and I let the project develop freely and spontaneously.

In sharing my process with you, I hope to give you permission to unlock your creative spirit. This book will help you take those adored fabrics and bring them to life in unique, vibrant, exciting quilts.

Many quilts need a little Fred Flintstone.

Use These Fabrics Too

The following types of fabrics are often found in my work, and each does a special job in a quilt.

The bright blue is a real zinger next to all the green and orange.

zingers

To me, a zinger is an unusual color, image, or unexpected motif. A zinger is often not noticed at first and is discovered as the viewer spends more time looking at the work. It adds interest and whimsy. I think anything that makes people stop and say, "Oh, look at that," is a zinger, and I highly recommend adding zingers wherever you can. My *Modern Home Landscape* (page 73) quilt has some zingery red fabric with white polka dots, but it also has Fred Flintstone peeking out somewhere. A strategically placed Elvis or Disney character can never go awry. I like to make my quilts fun to look at as well as beautiful.

A little dog is hiding in this strip; see it?

eye rests

A lot is made of giving the eye a place to "rest" on a busy quilt. The idea is that if the quilt pattern or fabrics have a lot going on, then a simple block or fabric is needed to give the eye a place to stop and focus. I'm not so sure about this. Yes, you should avoid having your quilt designs look chaotic, but restfulness can come from repetition of a theme or motif. Look at *Fly By the Garden* (page 23) to see that in the chaos of the color, the structure created by the repeating triangles gives the eye an anchor.

Cutting a single fabric and sandwiching other fabrics or blocks in the middle of the pieces can give continuity to a quilt and can create a visual connection or calmness that can work in place of an "eye rest." Alternately, careful use of stripes can create the calming effect sometimes needed in an active quilt.

Of course, you can always rest your eyes when you're asleep!

use white

I think it is essential in a quilt to have a little spot, or two or three, of white. White relieves any flatness or dullness in a quilt and gives a sparkle to the work that no other color can do. I am always looking for fabrics that have white in them and am sure to add them to each quilt.

Fabrics without any white

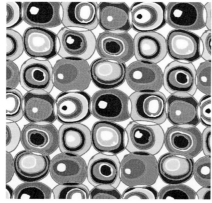 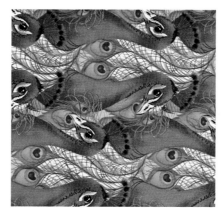 

White in a fabric gives a little sparkle.

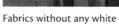

light givers

A fabric that has light, medium, and dark in it is sometimes called a light giver. The combination of the three color values in a fabric is often used by a designer to create curves or to give depth to a composition. Strategic use of light givers can break up sections of a quilt that read solid from a distance and can help create more visual interest. Try it!

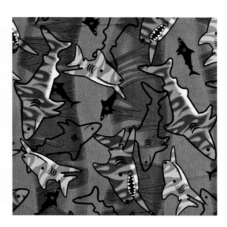

Light seems to shine through these fabrics with the combination of light, medium, and dark colors.

Alter That Fabric

I use altered fabrics in many of my quilts. Here are some ways to add that maverick touch.

making fabric wider (or longer)

Sometimes you may need to extend a fabric and make it wider (or longer). Because borders are usually much longer than the usable width of fabric, you often need to join fabric pieces to make a border strip that is long enough. I like to use a technique, especially with novelty prints, that makes a long, continuous strip of fabric without an obvious seam.

Making a piece of fabric wider using fabrics that have a definite print or stripe is a challenge, but with a little practice, you can achieve perfection. Take the steps slowly, double-check before you cut, and don't do it late at night!

1. Place a cut piece of fabric (A) directly on top of an identical section of fabric (B). Align the design motifs exactly. Cut the bottom layer of fabric into a strip using the top and bottom edges of the top fabric as a guide.

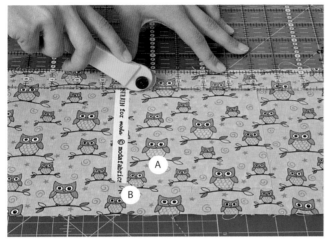

Make a matching-width strip by aligning one piece on top of another and cut top and bottom.

Left: A busy spot is a bad choice for a join. Right: Choose a plain spot for a better join. (Note: Dark line shown for clarity. Lightly draw your line to keep it from showing through fabrics.)

tip . . . .

Since designs repeat differently with each fabric, yardage requirements may not be enough to accommodate the number of identical cuts needed for a given project. This is especially true for larger print fabrics. If you find you don't have enough fabric to cut the required number of identical strips for a particular project, you may need to purchase more fabric or piece the fabrics in a pleasing arrangement to get the required length (see Fabric Requirements, page 14).

3. Use a ruler to make a clean cut ¼" outside the drawn line.

4. Stack 2 strips (A and B), with piece (A) on top. Align the layered motifs exactly.

5. Position a ruler with the ½" line along the clean-cut edge of the top fabric (A). Hold the ruler in place and remove the top fabric (A).

Overlap the fabrics and lay the ½" ruler line on the edge of the top fabric, and then remove (A).

2. Locate a place to make the join in the piece to extend (A). Look for a spot that will not be too obvious and that is fairly plain with few or no design elements. Use a ruler and a pencil, chalk, or water-soluble marker to lightly draw a perpendicular line that intersects this section of fabric.

6. Cut the bottom fabric (B) along the ruler edge.

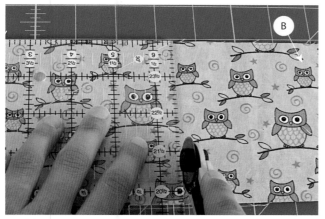

Cut (B) along ruler edge.

7. Pin the layers, right sides together, along the newly cut edges. Sew the layers using a ¼" seam allowance. Do not backstitch. Press the seam open to help the join lie flat and disappear.

If the pieces are not matching well, adjust the seam allowance or add a smidge to the cutting line.

This seam was too fat.

This seam was too thin.

This seam is just right.

tips

- If you think your join looks bad, hang the offending piece on your design wall and walk 6 feet away. If it still bothers you, it will probably always bother you; so fix it. If it doesn't jump out at you, it is likely that no one else will ever see it; so leave it.

- If the seam is obvious or ugly, a bridging piece—like a flower or leaf from the fabric—can be appliquéd to the top. This serves to cover some of the seam and create visual continuity.

Selective Cutting

One of the most delightful things to do is to discover fabrics within fabrics. When shopping, try to look beyond the patterns and motifs to see hidden shapes, curves, and stripes. The opportunities afforded in each fabric can yield happy surprises and can solve problems in quilts. Finding interesting shapes, creating your own curves, or getting a cool stripe out of a print makes you feel like the master of the quilt!

removing motifs

Sometimes a fabric works in a quilt, except for a part that you don't like. Consider using a fabric with an undesirable color or part by removing the unwanted portion. Cut out the unwanted area, leaving a ¼" seam allowance in the remaining fabric. Sew the remaining pieces of fabric together.

Cut to remove unwanted motif.

New fabric with unwanted motif removed

making stripes

You can make stripes out of many kinds of fabric. One way is to use a large print fabric and cut off sections of the printed design to create unusual stripes. Save the leftovers; they could be just the exact piece you need for another project.

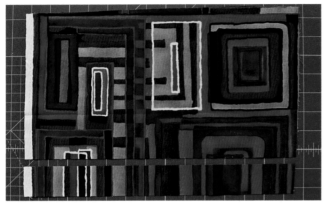

Turn squares into stripes.

Horizontal, vertical, and diagonal cuts can yield very interesting results.

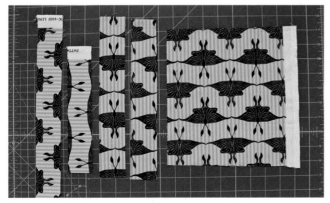

One fabric can give very different images.

creating curves

A great way to add movement to a quilt and give lines that the eye can dance across is to use fabric that has curves or that is cut curvy. Using curvy fabric can also give the illusion of a more complicated design, just by the fabric's pattern. Fussy cutting or carving (see below) the shape out of the fabric are two ways to make the curves work for you.

Each cut of the fabric will yield different results. Horizontal and vertical cuts can create completely different looks.

To create long strips of curves, choose visual reference points to align the ruler; then make the cuts along the same reference point each time. Keep in mind that lengthwise (parallel to the selvage) cuts have less stretch and should be sewn on top when joining to other fabrics (see Making Friends with the Feed Dogs, page 15).

Curves cut with different reference points create movement and visual interest.

carved curves

Carved pieces are easy to create and make the quilt look really great. Carved borders can be fussy cut from curvy fabric by cutting along the curved lines of the design and then appliquéd in place. They can also be wavy cut with a rotary cutter and pieced to the adjoining fabric (see Jalousie, Borders page 57).

Carved borders create a dynamic edge for a quilt.

inserting strips

There are occasions when your fabric, border piece, sashing, or stripe just needs a little touch of something else. Perhaps you need a little bit of color or a break in the pattern. You can sneak other pieces in wherever you need them. Simply piece in another fabric and press the seams open.

Yellow squares were inserted in this border to create a visual break.

Raw-Edge Appliqué

Leaving the edges of your pieces raw and topstitching them onto the quilt has become an accepted way to work. It gives an "artsy" feel to the work. I often temporarily hold raw-edged appliqué pieces in place using a water-soluble gluestick and pressing with a hot, dry iron. The heat from the iron dries the glue, allowing me to quickly position the appliqué. The glue will come out of the quilt with washing.

The glued appliqué pieces are then permanently stitched in place either with an appliqué stitch that covers the raw edges or during the quilting process. Leaving the edges unfinished allows the fabric to unravel and creates texture. So decide how much fraying you want around the appliqué edges and plan the quilt accordingly.

Maverick Quilter Says

If you blow it when you are altering fabric, just use it anyway! I cut this long vertical strip in the wrong place and sewed it back together. Don't tell anyone.

Seam

If you make a cutting mistake, even on a large-scale print, it isn't all that obvious. Sew it back together and move on.

sew that fabric: *quilting basics*

Fabric Requirements

Most fabrics come 43" to 45" wide, but most of the yardage requirements given in this book allow for 40" of usable fabric design, with exceptions clearly noted in the projects (Lovely Landscape, page 73, is an exception). The fabrics needed for each project are listed in the chapters. Extra yardage has been added to the requirements to allow for cutting errors. However, If you have been quilting for a while, I encourage you to go "shopping" from your own stash and pull out bits and pieces that might work.

As noted in the project instructions, for the quilts that use very large motifs or very large pieces of fabrics, you might want to purchase extra. This will allow you to use the best area of the fabric design for your quilt. It also allows you the option of fussy cutting and gives you extra in case of a cutting or sewing error.

The tight weave of the selvage (the factory edge of the fabric) will not respond to washing, sewing, or quilting as the rest of the fabric will. Remove it whenever possible to prevent problems.

note

The selvage is a great source of information, and the little color dots can aid you in understanding the colors and hues that might go with each piece of fabric. It can also contain the fabric name, designer, pattern number, or manufacturer. Removing a sample of the selvage with the information and keeping it for future use can be helpful.

Seam Allowances and Sewing

Where sewing is required, the cutting sizes are designed for ¼" seam allowances. You can certainly sew wonky if you want; just make the blocks a little larger and take the time to trim to size and square things up when joining blocks and borders. This will help make the quilt come together successfully. If you want to let go of the rules and use a funky sewing style, I am not going to scold you!

I don't usually backstitch when piecing, because eventually I'll stitch across the seam when adding more pieces, which secures the stitches in place. I do, however, backstitch when I add the final borders, because these are the final seams of the quilt top. The seams won't be crossed by other piecing, and the edges will be pulled or manipulated while quilting. Backstitching on the borders secures the seams so they won't pull apart.

Chain sewing when possible helps reduce bunching and thread tangles at the beginning and end of the sewing. Separate the chained pieces by cutting the connector threads.

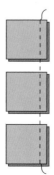

Chain sew off one piece and on to the next.

Making Friends with the Feed Dogs

Those little canine teeth on your machine can wreak havoc with your project, so it is imperative that you understand them. During each stitch, the feed dogs pull the fabric toward the back of the presser foot when the needle is lifted.

On most machines, the length of each pull is directed by the stitch length value—the smaller the number, the shorter the stitch. With the presser foot pushing down, the feed dogs can actually pull the bottom layer of fabric at a different rate than the top fabric. With a small piece or block, the difference is negligible. The amount of pull can vary and be significant, however, when sewing larger pieces or blocks and when sewing fabrics that are cut crosswise (selvage to selvage) or on the bias. Pinning the fabrics together helps keep the feed dogs at bay by keeping the fabrics together as you sew. The larger the piece, the more pins are required. Here are some guidelines:

1. Always measure large pieces and cut them to the same measurement before pinning and joining.

2. Always place fabrics that have been cut lengthwise (parallel to the selvages) on top of fabrics cut crosswise (from selvage to selvage), if possible.

3. Always place fabrics cut on the bias on the top, if possible.

4. If joining two bias cuts, line them up at the edges, but pin only at the center and end points. Gently push the layered fabrics toward the presser foot during sewing, letting the feed dogs do most of the work so there is minimal tension on the bottom piece.

5. When joining a set of blocks to a long piece of sashing, place the sashing on top. Use the guidelines in Measure, Pin, and Sew (page 19).

Lacing the Blocks Together

Once the blocks are pieced, it's time to sew them together using the lacing method.

1. Lay out your blocks in the order that they will appear in the finished quilt top.

2. Starting with Row 1, chain sew (page 14) Block 2 to Block 1. Then sew Block 2 to Block 1 from Row 2. Continue this process for Blocks 1 and 2 for all rows. Press the seams of each row in alternate directions to help them nest together when you sew the rows together.

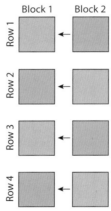

Sew Block 2 to Block 1.

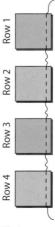

Chain sew.

3. Add Block 3 to Block 2 for each row.

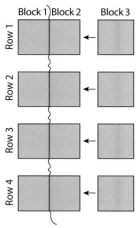

Chain sew Block 3 to Block 2.

4. Continue this process of adding each sequential set of blocks to the rows until all the blocks have been sewn in place. Leave the connector threads attached.

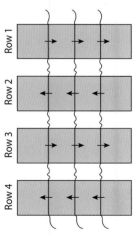

Press seams of each row, alternating directions.

5. Nest the seams, pin them, and then sew the rows together.

Cutting

rotary cutting

The quilts in this book are cut with a rotary cutter and ruler on a self-healing mat. Unless noted, each piece is cut selvage to selvage and subcut after removing the selvages.

crosswise cutting

Crosswise cutting refers to fabric cut across the grain from selvage to selvage. It has some stretch to it because of the way it is woven. Keep this in mind when sewing long pieces, since they can stretch a little and get longer. Pinning pieces together helps eliminate this (see Making Friends with the Feed Dogs, page 15).

lengthwise cutting

Lengthwise cutting refers to fabric that is cut parallel to the selvage edges. It has very little stretch, if any at all.

cutting sashings, borders, and backing

Depending on your sewing style, the blocks you make may be a different size than the project instructions indicate. So hold off cutting the sashings, borders, or backing pieces until the adjoining pieced units are made and can be accurately measured. Wait until the blocks are made, pressed, and trimmed to the same size before you measure and cut the sashings. Then sew the whole quilt center together, press, and square it up before you measure and cut the borders. For the projects in this book, I supplied extra cutting length for the sashing and borders. This way when you're ready to attach them, they can easily be trimmed to fit to the actual measurements of the quilt.

Pressing

pressing surface

I find that an ironing board is too soft and curvy for me, so I have created a firm, flat ironing surface by putting a low-nap towel over a plywood board. I use hook-and-loop tape on the corners to hold the towel in place, which makes it easy to remove the towel for washing when it gets dirty.

pressing seams

Use pressing to your advantage. After sewing the pieces, iron the seams flat while the pieced fabrics are still stacked and facing right sides together. This is called setting the seams. Next, open the pieced unit, right sides up, and press the seam flat while guiding the seam allowance toward the direction indicated in the project. If necessary, gently pull the fabric while pressing to make adjustments to the shape of the pieced unit or block. I use steam when I press, which helps relax the fabrics into their new shape, and then set them nicely as they dry.

Bias-cut edges, such as in triangles, stretch and distort easily. When pressing bias seams, go slowly and handle them gently to avoid distorting the shape or stretching the seam.

If you have the time and patience, let the pressed seams cool in place on the ironing board to help the project stay flat.

Pinning

To pin or not to pin—that is the question. Pin when you think it will help you sew. Pin if you think it makes the blocks come out better and when you join large pieces together. Always pin borders to the quilt top before sewing. For more detailed information on adding borders and long sashings, see Measure, Pin, and Sew (page 19).

Borders

Borders are definitely one of the most important parts of a quilt. When adding a border, the size, color, and level of complexity are all choices that can affect the overall composition of the quilt. Borders can serve as a frame around the piece, giving the center of the quilt a definite edge, or they can recede into the background. Consider your choices to select a border fabric, width, and level of complexity that best produces the effect you're trying to achieve.

note

I like using medium- to large-scale prints for my border fabrics. These fabrics tend to have designs that run parallel to the selvage edges and are referred to as lengthwise directional prints. Keeping the orientation of the design consistent throughout the quilt is important when using these busy fabrics. Pay special attention to the instructions for projects that use these fabrics. Quilts using these prints need to have the side borders and vertical sashing cut lengthwise to keep the fabric design running vertically on the finished quilt.

Notice the vertical orientation of the fabric and how the geishas are all facing upright.

With each project in this book, feel free to change the borders to your liking. Making the borders larger or smaller than the stated size is an easy way to change the size of the quilt.

the effect of color choice

One of the most important things to consider when choosing a border is the effect the color (or colors) will have on the overall look of the quilt. In many quilts, the border fabric amounts to the largest piece of fabric. The border color informs the eye that the quilt you are looking at is *that* color. For instance, if you put a wide gray border on a gray, purple, and white quilt, the viewer's eye will register it as a "gray" quilt. Similarly, if the same quilt has a purple border, the viewer takes away the idea that the quilt is a "purple" quilt, even if there are other colors in the center. There is nothing wrong with this, but just keep it in mind in your planning.

you must measure and pin borders

Whether your border is one piece or a patchwork of blocks, there is one cardinal rule to adding borders: Measure and pin! No, no, no, Virginia, you can't just plunk the quilt top onto the border, sew, and trim the excess! This leads to two of the worst things that can happen to the quilt:

1. The center ends up smaller than the borders, which provides excess fabric in the borders. This excess makes the borders ruffle and become wavy because they are bigger than the whole quilt—very bad. It also makes the quilt very hard to quilt. The final results nullify all the good work you did in making the quilt center.

2. Alternately, the center can end up bigger than the borders. This makes the middle of the quilt bow out and balloon up. You will end up having to quilt in tucks and lumps and bumps of fabric in an attempt to wrangle the quilt center down inside the small borders.

Consider yourself warned!

measure, pin, and sew

Quilt centers are not always perfectly square; either side of a quilt might be a different length than the middle. By cutting the borders to length using the center measurement, the inherent imperfection is balanced out when the border is sewn to the quilt. Follow these steps to add borders:

1. Press the quilt center and square it up, smoothing it flat and trimming it around the sides and all 4 corners.

2. Measure vertically through the center of the quilt and trim the first 2 borders to this size.

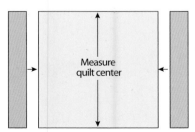

Measure quilt center and make borders that size.

3. At this point, the borders might be a little longer than the quilt top, or the quilt top might be a little longer than the border. Place whichever piece is the longer piece as the bottom layer, next to the feed dogs.

4. Pin the borders to each side of the quilt center. Pin each end of the border first; then place one pin in the middle. Insert the pins facing the sewing line but not touching it.

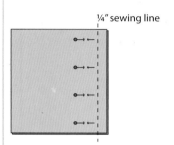

¼" sewing line

Pin toward sewing line.

5. Add more pins between each set of existing pins, while smoothing and adjusting the layers of fabric. Add enough pins until the layers of fabric sit flat and you can produce a nice flat seam.

6. Stitch the seam with the pins on top, backstitching at the beginning and end. Gently push the fabric, letting the feed dogs help gather any extra fabric on the bottom layer. Press the seam toward the border.

7. Repeat the process for the remaining 2 borders, measuring horizontally through the center of the quilt with the side borders attached. Cut the borders to this size, pin, sew, and press. Voilà!

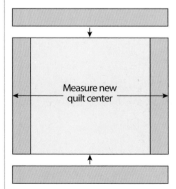

Measure new quilt center

Measure new quilt dimensions, including borders, and trim borders to size.

Backing

Make the backing a minimum of 4″ longer and wider than the quilt top. Piece, if necessary, trimming off the selvages before you piece to the desired size. Sew the seams.

To economize, piece the back from any leftover quilting fabrics or blocks in your collection. Patchwork backs get noticed and they are a fun way to use up extra fabric. To be sure that the backing will lie nice and flat, follow Making Fabric Wider (or Longer), page 9. Resist the temptation to just sew all the raw edges together willy-nilly. Trust me; it is worth the extra time to reduce headaches later!

Batting

The type of batting to use is a personal decision. Experiment to find the one you like best.

Cut batting approximately 4″ longer and wider than your quilt top. Note that your batting choice will affect how much quilting is necessary for the quilt. Follow the manufacturer's instructions to find out the maximum distance needed between lines of quilting.

Layering

1. Smooth out the quilt backing, wrong side up, and tape the edges down to a flat surface with masking tape. (If you are working on carpet, you can use T-pins to secure the backing to the carpet.)

2. Center the batting on top, smoothing out any folds.

3. Place the quilt top, right side up, on top of the batting and backing, making sure it is centered.

Basting

Basting keeps the quilt layers from shifting while you are quilting.

If you plan to machine quilt, pin baste the quilt layers with safety pins placed a minimum of 3″–4″ apart. Begin basting in the center and move toward the edges, first in vertical, then horizontal rows. Try not to pin directly on the intended quilting lines.

If you plan to hand quilt, baste the layers together with thread, using a long needle and light-colored thread. Knot one end of the thread. Using stitches approximately the length of the needle, begin in the center and move out toward the edges in vertical and horizontal rows, approximately 4″ apart. Add two diagonal rows of basting.

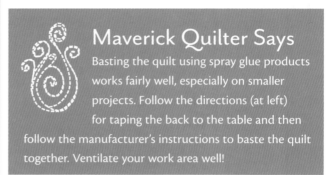

Maverick Quilter Says

Basting the quilt using spray glue products works fairly well, especially on smaller projects. Follow the directions (at left) for taping the back to the table and then follow the manufacturer's instructions to baste the quilt together. Ventilate your work area well!

Quilting

Quilting, whether by hand or by machine, enhances the design of the quilt. You may choose to quilt in-the-ditch, echo the motifs, use designs from quilting books and stencils, or do your own free-motion quilting. Remember to check your batting manufacturer's instructions to find out the maximum distance needed between lines of quilting.

This is the time to make sure that any raw-edge appliqué is stitched down well. The quilting can trace around the edges or go back and forth over them.

Having your quilting done by a professional quilter is a real luxury. The stitching and designs are really wonderful, and, best of all, you don't have to do it yourself. Consider sending out your special projects to a trusted professional and sit back, relax, and wait for the magic. With no more backaches and neck cricks, it might be the best money you ever spend! Before you send out the quilt, check with the quilter for batting and backing requirements; they may vary from home-sewing requirements.

Binding

Binding adds the finishing touch to your quilt. Choose a contrasting binding fabric to add another design element to your quilt or a matching fabric to have the binding recede into the background. On my quilts, I prefer using a ¼" double-fold straight-grain binding.

double-fold straight-grain binding

Before adding the binding, trim the excess batting and backing from the quilt, even with the edges of the quilt top. Square up the corners and even out the sides if they are distorted from the quilting.

1. For a ¼" finished binding, cut the binding strips 2½" wide and piece them together with diagonal seams to make a continuous binding strip. Trim the seam allowance to ¼". Press the seams open.

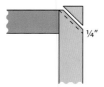

Sew from corner to corner.

Trim seam allowance to ¼".

2. Press the entire strip in half lengthwise with wrong sides together, aligning the raw edges.

3. With the raw edges even, pin the binding to the front edge of the quilt a few inches away from the corner, leaving the first few inches of the binding unattached.

4. Sew the binding to the quilt, using a ¼" seam allowance and leaving the starting end unattached. Stop sewing ¼" away from the first corner and backstitch one stitch.

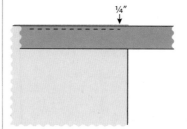

Stitch to ¼" from corner.

> ## Maverick Quilter Says
>
> I sew my bindings on with the quilt facing down and the binding underneath, against the feed dogs. This gives a little more fabric to the binding and keeps the tension nice. Although you can pin the binding before sewing, I find it works equally well to sew the binding without pinning.

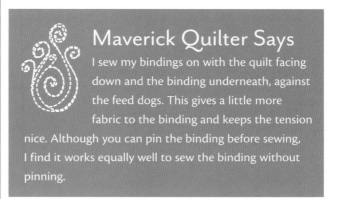

5. Lift the presser foot and needle. Rotate the quilt one-quarter turn. Fold the binding at a right angle so it extends straight above the quilt and the fold forms a 45° angle in the corner.

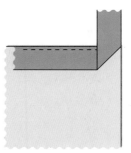

First fold for miter

6. Bring the binding strip down even with the edge of the quilt. Pin the binding in place.

7. Sew the next side, starting with a backstitch ¼" away from the folded corner and ending ¼" away from the next corner. Sew the corners, as before. Repeat this process for the remaining sides, stopping several inches from the unattached starting tail.

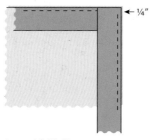
← ¼"

Second fold alignment

8. Fold the ending tail of the binding back on itself where it meets the beginning binding tail. From the fold, measure and mark 2½". Cut the ending binding tail along the marked line.

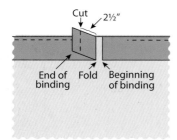
Cut   2½"

End of   Fold   Beginning
binding   of binding

Cut binding tail.

9. Open both tails. Place one tail on top of the other tail at right angles, right sides together. Mark a diagonal line from corner to corner and stitch on the line. Check that you've done it correctly and that the binding fits the quilt, and then trim the seam allowance to ¼". Press open.

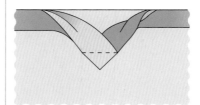

Stitch ends of binding diagonally.

10. Refold the binding and stitch this section in place on the quilt. Press the binding away from the quilt. Fold the binding over the raw edges to the quilt back and then hand or machine stitch the binding in place.

tip . . . .

Skip the binding! For small quilts, it is easy to do this. Spray baste the batting and fix a piece of backing the same size as the quilt top, right side up. Place the quilt on the backing, right sides together. Pin in place and stitch a ¼" seam around the quilt top. Stop sewing 6" from the start, leaving an opening. Trim off the corners, being careful not to clip the seams. Turn the project right side out through the opening. Press well and sew the opening closed. At this point you can quilt or tie the project. Try it; you might just like it. I even quilt these kinds of projects on the longarm sewing machine with good results!

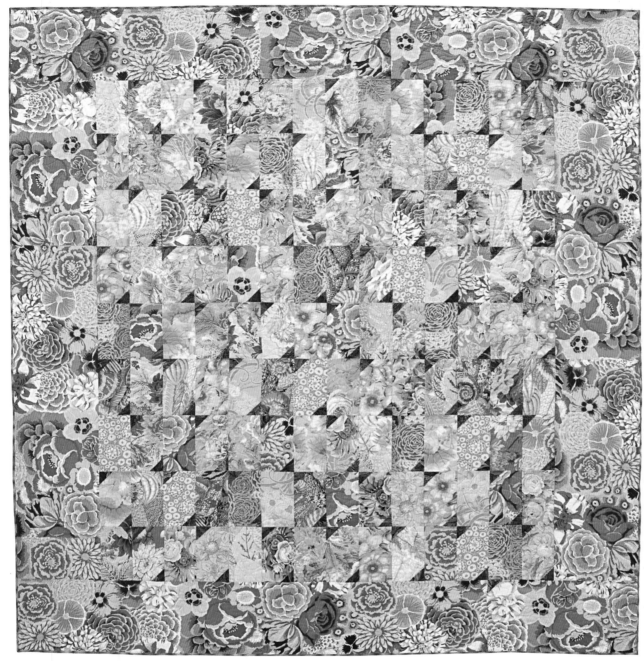

Fly By the Garden, made by Alethea Ballard

fly by

Showcase those gorgeous prints in this easy queen-size bed quilt. With all the medium-value florals available, collecting fabric for this quilt is easy. Use a wild selection to make an even more dynamic quilt. Get a highly contrasting color that really pops for the triangle "butterflies."

The Fly By design is quite simple to construct. Using large rectangles and straight seams, it is a good project for a beginner. This large,

dramatic quilt looks wonderful on a bed and can totally change the feel in a room. Whether you are choosing bright, colorful florals or dark batiks, the corner-triangle "butterflies" add a sense of whimsy and movement across the surface.

Notice how inserting a few triangles into the border piecing ties the center and border together.

use that fabric: *big florals!*

Use those jumbo- and large-size florals—the bigger the better. Quilters are always looking for ways to use all of the supersize flowers that are available right now. One way to see a lot of a giant print is in a wide border. Using large-size prints for the center of a quilt gives the viewer's eye lots to look at, and the overall result makes a powerful statement.

materials

medium-scale prints for blocks

- ⅝ yard each of 8 different fabrics or ⅓ yard each of 16 different fabrics (Note: These are minimum requirements. Purchase extra, if desired, for cutting errors.)

high-contrast print for corner triangles

- ¾ yard

borders

- 3⅜ yards

binding

- ⅞ yard
(can be same fabric as border)

backing

- 7½ yards

batting

- 91″ × 97″

cutting

medium-scale prints

- Cut a total of 16 strips 8½″ × width of fabric.

Subcut the strips into 126 rectangles 5″ × 8½″ for the blocks.

contrasting print

- Cut 9 strips 2½″ × width of fabric.

Subcut the strips into 130 squares 2½″ × 2½″ for the corner triangles.

border

These border cutting measurements assume accurate piecing of the quilt top. To avoid errors, cut the border strips after piecing the top and double-checking the measurements against the quilt assembly diagram (page 26).

- Cut 4 strips 12½″ × width of fabric. Cut 3 of the strips to measure as follows: 40½″*, 32½″, and 24½″ for the side borders. Sew the leftover from the 24½″ strip to the remaining full strip, press the seam, and cut to measure 48½″ long.

- Cut 5 strips 11″ × width of fabric for the top and bottom borders. Cut 2 of the strips to measure as follows: 35″ and 21½″. Sew the leftover from the 21½″ strip to another full strip, press the seam, and cut to measure 53″. Sew the remaining 2 strips together, press the seam, and cut to measure 66½″.

binding

- Cut 10 strips 2½″ × width of fabric.

note

* Indicates a dimension larger than the 40″ of usable yardage used in the book. If you can squeeze out the extra yardage from your strips, then that's good. If you can't get it, you will need to sew on an extra piece to make the strip equal to that length.

Blocks

Use ¼" seam allowances unless otherwise noted.

1. Divide the rectangles into 2 piles of 63, distributing the fabrics so that each pile has an equal amount of each print. Set aside one pile for later.

2. Draw a line from corner to corner on the 2½" corner-triangle squares. Place a square on one corner of a rectangle and sew along the marked line.

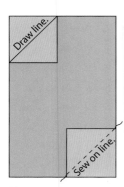

Place square on corner and sew on line.

3. Trim the corner, leaving a ¼" seam allowance. Press the seam toward the rectangle. Add another corner triangle to the opposite corner, in the same manner.

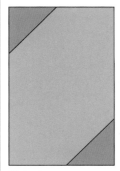

Trim.

4. Repeat to make 63 corner-triangle blocks.

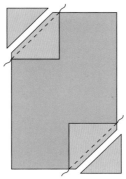

Make 63.

Quilt Assembly

1. Lay out all the blocks on a design surface, alternating the 63 plain rectangles with the 63 corner-triangle blocks.

2. Lace the rows together (page 16).

3. Press the seams, alternating the direction for each row.

4. Sew the rows together. Press.

Borders

For more detailed information about adding borders, see Measure, Pin, and Sew, page 19.

1. Lay out the border pieces and sew the corner triangles to the 4 pieces as shown in the quilt assembly diagram (page 26).

2. Sew the border pieces together to make the top, bottom, and side borders.

3. Add the side borders to the quilt top and then the top and bottom borders, pressing the seam toward the border.

Finishing

Layer, quilt, and bind your quilt (pages 20–21).

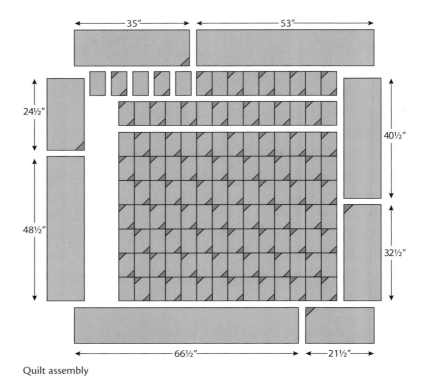

Quilt assembly

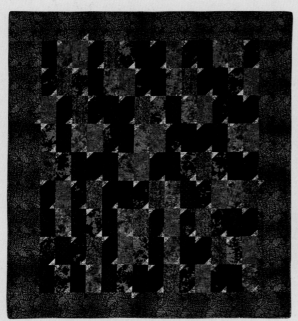

Fly By Night, made by Alethea Ballard, machine quilted by Sandy Klop

I was looking for a masculine feel when I made a quilt for my son's eighteenth birthday. His favorite color is blue, so this great collection of batiks seemed the perfect choice. I had a little fun when piecing the borders and repositioned some of the "butterfly" triangle pieces. This quilt looks really beautiful on the bed, and the deep color creates a very calming feel for the room.

use that fabric: *batiks!*

Use those batik fabrics. Batiks can be very versatile in a quilt. The pattern and colors are usually the same on both the front and the back of the fabric. This means you never have to worry about using up the good side, which can be especially trouble free for paper piecing and raw-edge appliqué. The rich, dense colors can be blended within a quilt to achieve the most wonderful and subtle results!

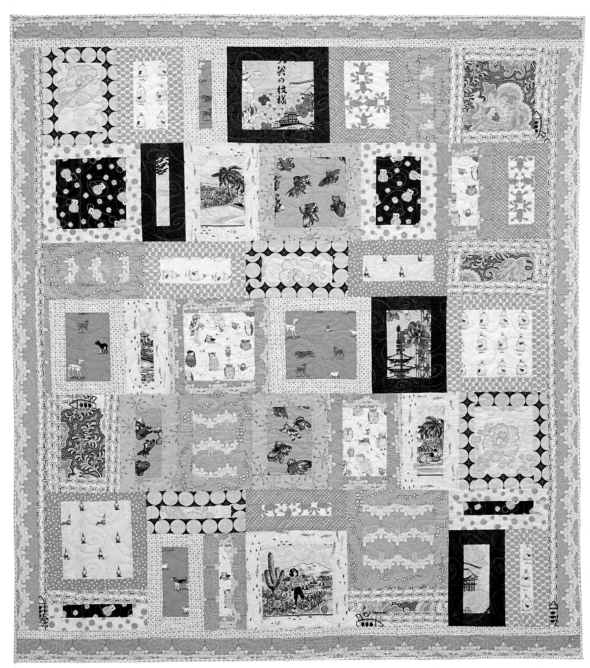

Show Off Summer, made by Alethea Ballard

FINISHED BLOCK: Various   **FINISHED QUILT:** 65" × 76½"

show off

Show off those medium- and small-motif fabrics that feature charming images that captivate you. Fabric designers are really having fun creating a cornucopia of creatures, flowers, and humorous images. These are called conversation or novelty prints, and if they have been talking to you, then this quilt is for you.

The block frames are really fun because you can use smaller-motif novelty prints instead of solid fabrics. Keep in mind that the block frames touch each other, so avoid getting fabrics that are too similar to each other for the frames.

Whether choosing a variety of florals, paisleys, and dots, like in *Show Off Jewels* (page 30) or funny conversation prints, like in *Show Off Summer* (above), this quilt design is fun to work on and beautiful to make. It is easier than it looks—try it!

materials

large novelty prints for block centers

- Fat eighth, fat quarter, or ¼ yard cuts of 12 different fabrics

small novelty prints for block frames

- ⅜ yard each of 12 different fabrics

inner border

- ¼ yard each of 2 fabrics

outer border

- ½ yard each of 2 fabrics

binding

- ⅔ yard

backing

- 4 yards

batting

- 69″ × 81″

cutting

large novelty prints

- Cut all 12 pieces to measure 8½″ × 20″ for the block centers.

small novelty prints

- Cut 4 strips 2¼″ × width of fabric from *each* of the 12 fabrics for the frame strips.

Subcut each set of 4 matching strips as follows:

Cut 1 strip into 2 pieces 2¼″ × 20″.

Cut the remaining 3 strips into a total of 8 pieces 2¼″ × 12″.

Keep the leftovers and sew the ends together for extra frames, if needed.

inner border

- Cut 4 strips 1½″ × width of fabric from each of the 2 fabrics.

outer border

- Cut 4 strips 3¼″ × width of fabric from each of the 2 fabrics.

binding

- Cut 8 strips 2½″ × width of fabric.

Maverick Quilter Says

Let's face it: sewing is not exactly a cheap sport. If you're like me (and if you're reading this book, you probably are; heaven help us all), then you buy fabric when you really love it. Over time you have likely collected quite a pile of novelty prints. On the other hand, if you have held off on buying those talkative fabrics because you didn't know what to do with them, I say go forth and buy! You don't have to know what you are doing when you buy the fabric. It will talk to you and tell you what to do in time. Yes, you *are* hearing voices. While your stash of novelty prints might be a strange, mismatched, eclectic collection, it is *your* collection, and it is time to show it off.

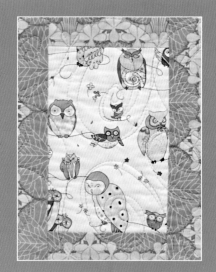

Blocks

Use ¼" seam allowances unless otherwise noted.

1. Sew a 2¼" × 20" frame strip to each long side of an 8½" × 20" block center piece, sewing with the frame strip against the feed dogs. Press seams toward the block center. Repeat to make 12 block center strip sets that measure 12" × 20".

2. Make 1 each of Blocks A, B, C, and D by selecting 4 block center strip sets and cutting each of the following pieces from a different strip set, saving the leftovers for Step 4:

   1 piece 7½" × 12" (Block A)

   1 piece 5" × 12" (Block B)

   1 piece 4½" × 12" (Block C)

   1 piece 3" × 12" (Block D)

3. Subcut each of the 8 remaining 12" × 20" strips into 4 pieces, as follows:

   1 piece 8½" × 12" (Block E)

   1 piece 5½" × 12" (Block F)

   1 piece 3½" × 12" (Block G)

   1 piece 2" × 12" (Block H)

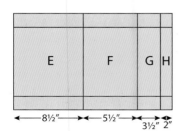

Cut strip set into 4 pieces.

4. Cut the following from the leftover strip sets from Step 2, cutting the larger pieces from the largest leftovers first:

   2 pieces 8½" × 12" (Block E)

   1 piece 5½" × 12" (Block F)

   3 pieces 3½" × 12" (Block G)

   2 pieces 2" × 12" (Block H)

tip . . . .

After cutting all the strip sets as directed, you should have the following block pieces:

   1 each of Blocks A, B, C, and D

   9 of Block F

   10 each of Blocks E and H

   11 of Block G

5. Sew a matching 2¼" × 12" frame strip to each side of each of Blocks A through H. Press toward the center.

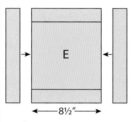

Add frame strips to complete blocks.

tip . . . .

For the flattest possible blocks, sew the center pieces to the frames with the frame strips on the bottom against the feed dogs. If you don't do this, you might find that the centers bow out in the middle.

Quilt Assembly

1. Lay out all of the blocks on a design surface, following the quilt assembly diagram (page 30).

2. Sew the blocks into rows. Press.

3. Sew the rows together. Press.

Borders

For more detailed information about adding borders, see Measure, Pin, and Sew, page 19.

1. Remove the selvage edges from the inner and outer border strips. Sew each strip, end to end, to its matched pair, making 4 inner and 4 outer border strips. Press.

2. Make the 4 borders by sewing each 1½″ inner border to a 3¼″ outer border piece along the long edge. Press.

3. Measure vertically through the center of the quilt top and cut the 2 side strips to length.

4. Sew the side strips to the quilt. Press.

5. Measure horizontally through the center of the quilt top, including the side borders, and cut the top and bottom strips to that length.

6. Sew the top and bottom borders to the quilt. Press.

Finishing

Layer, quilt, and bind your quilt (pages 20–21).

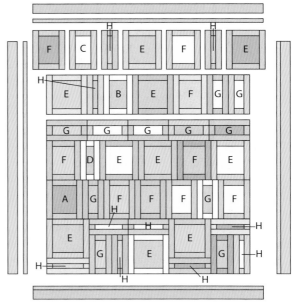

Quilt assembly

---

use that fabric: *white!*

Use more white! Fabrics with a white background can be hard to find, but they do wonders in a quilt. I snap them up whenever I can. White in a quilt makes it look young and fresh. It adds zing and pop, and brightens it up!

Show Off Jewels, made by Alethea Ballard

Really? Could I be more in love with this quilt? When I was at the store looking at all the yummy fabrics, the Show Off design came to mind, since it is a perfect way to use the bright florals and paisleys. The polka dots, small flowers, and dark fabrics in the borders really made it exciting to work on. I was able to use the leftover fabric to create a cool duvet cover. So clever!

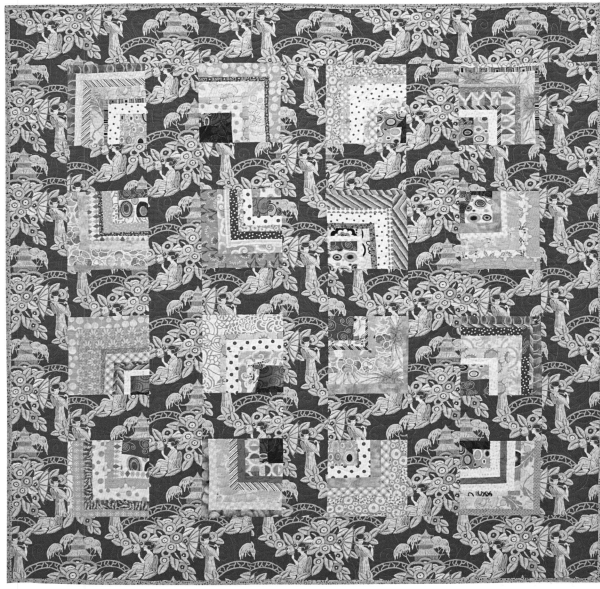

Geisha Housetop, made by Alethea Ballard

california housetop

Quilters often get their inspiration from old quilts, and the work of the quilters from Gee's Bend has been a rich source of creative sparks for many of us. The women from this remote community designed and made wonderful quilts. Their work has a sense of freedom from convention using an eclectic mix of fabrics. The design of this quilt is based on a very subtle, washed-out quilt that was made from feed sacks and pale cotton fabrics. How fun is it to take an exciting old block like the Housetop, which was used by the quilters from Gee's Bend, and give it a new life full of color, pattern, and whimsy? Tons and tons of fun!

In both *Geisha Housetop* (above) and *California Cars Housetop* (page 35), I was able to combine super color-saturated fabrics with strips of

similar colors, thus bringing a whole new feel to a very old quilt design. California Housetop uses a free construction style, is quick to make, and knocks the socks off everyone who sees it!

Three elements really make this quilt work: using interesting fabrics for each block's center to give each a clear focal point or anchor; using a single bridging color as the last strip on each block, which makes the blocks almost blend into the background fabric (in *Geisha Housetop* I used orange, and in *California Cars Housetop*, blue seemed the obvious choice); and putting a light fabric next to each center square. These light bits really help the centers dance. After that, the strips can just be any combination of alternating light and dark colors.

materials

lights, mediums, and darks for block strips

■ ⅛ yard pieces of 16 different fabrics in a variety of scales and textures, including stripes and dots

medium-scale prints for block centers

■ ⅜ yard or 16 scraps at least 4½" × 4½"

large-scale lengthwise-directional print for sashing and borders

■ 4 yards

binding

■ ⅔ yard

backing

■ 4½ yards

batting

■ 78" × 78"

cutting

lights, mediums, and darks

■ Cut 2 strips × width of fabric from *each* fabric, varying the width of each strip, for block stripes.

note

Vary the width of each strip. Example: From the first fabric, cut 1 strip 1½" wide and 1 strip 3" wide. From the second fabric, cut 1 strip 2" wide and 1 strip 2½" wide. From the third fabric, cut 1 strip 1¾" wide and 1 strip 2¾" wide, and so on. This will give you a great variety of sizes and add to the creative look of the project.

medium-scale prints

■ Cut 16 squares 4½" × 4½" for block centers.

large-scale print

■ Cut 2 identical strips 8½" × width of fabric for the top border. Join the strips to make 1 long continuous strip of fabric (see Making Fabric Wider [or Longer], page 9).

■ Cut 2 identical strips 8½" × width of fabric for the bottom border. Join the strips to make 1 long continuous strip of fabric.

■ Cut 4 strips 6½" × width of fabric.

Subcut the strips into a total of 12 rectangles 6½" × 10½" for the horizontal sashing.

■ Cut 1 piece 60" × width of fabric the side border and vertical sashing.

Remove the selvage from one edge. Subcut the piece following the cutting diagram (at right) and cutting the strips in this order—8", 7", 6", 7", 8"—to keep the continuity of the fabric design intact for the quilt assembly. See the Tip below to make the following:

2 pieces 8" × 60" for the side border

2 pieces 7" × 60" for the vertical sashing

1 piece 6" × 60" for the center vertical sashing

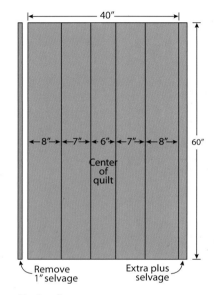

Cutting diagram

binding

■ Cut 8 strips 2½" × width of fabric.

tip

When working with a supersize print fabric, you want to see where the motifs are for the background pieces and visualize how they will look on the quilt. Audition them in place if you are unsure. Cut the top and bottom strips to avoid cutting off heads of creatures or slicing through centers of flowers and to get the images just where you want them. Yardage requirements for this quilt are generous to assist in aligning fabric designs.

use that fabric: *jumbo-size motifs!*

Giant cars, geishas, luscious landscapes, animals, flowers…where to begin? Don't be intimidated by the size of the motifs. All you have to do is find a quilt design that lets lots of the fabric show through. California Housetop is perfect for this. Now when you come across one of those jumbo-size images in fabric, you can snap it up. Get it! Use it!

Blocks

Use ¼" seam allowances unless otherwise noted.

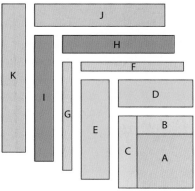

Block construction

Build the Housetop blocks from corner out.

1. Sew the first strip (B) to the top edge of the center block (A). Press toward the center block and trim off the excess.

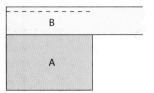

Add first strip.

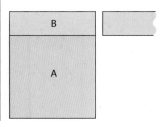

Press and trim.

Maverick Quilter Says

When using long vertical strips in a quilt, cut the strips to size in the same order that they are used in the quilt assembly. Number the strips, if necessary, to remember the order in which they were cut. Then, when assembling the quilt top, trim each strip to the length of the rows, measuring from the top edge. Doing this allows the fabric design to line up across the face of the quilt. So, even when blocks are sewn in between the vertical strips, the overall design has a sense of continuity, regularity, and harmony across the whole quilt (see Note, page 18).

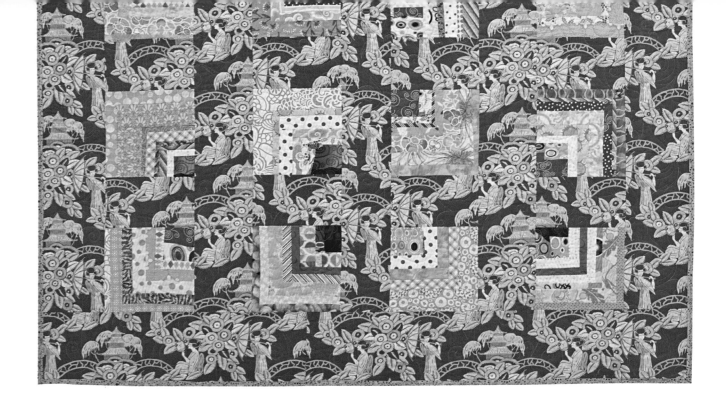

2. Add the same fabric (C) to the left side. Press toward the center block and trim. If desired, use strips of different widths when matching fabrics. This will add to the funkiness.

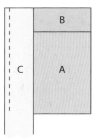

Add second strip.

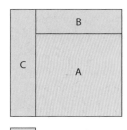

Press and trim.

3. Continue adding strips to the top and left sides, alternating fabric colors, scales, and strip widths until the block measures more than 10½″ × 10½″.

4. Press the block well.

5. Trim the block to measure 10½″ × 10½″. Since the blocks are oversized, they can be trimmed square to the center block or cut on an angle to get a funkier look to the quilt. Make 16.

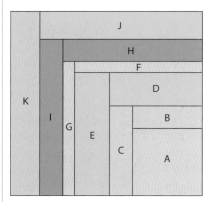

Make 16 randomly pieced blocks.

Quilt Assembly

1. Lay out all the blocks and horizontal sashing on a design surface following the quilt assembly diagram (page 35).

2. Sew the blocks and horizontal sashing together in vertical rows. Press toward the sashing.

3. Trim the vertical rows to the same 64½″ length.

Vertical Sashing and Borders

Sew the vertical sashing to the quilt in the same process as you used for adding a border. For more detailed information about adding borders, see Measure, Pin, and Sew, page 19.

1. Measure from the top edge and cut the vertical sashing strips and side border strips to the same length as the vertical rows (see Maverick Quilter Says, page 33).

2. Arrange the rows, vertical sashing, and side border strips on the design surface following the quilt assembly diagram (at right) and positioning the sashing and border strips in the same order as they were cut from the fabric (see the cutting diagram and Tip, page 32).

3. Pin and sew the rows, vertical sashing, and side borders together. Press.

4. Measure the finished width of the quilt top horizontally through the middle, including the side borders.

5. Trim the top and bottom borders to the length from Step 4 and sew them to the quilt top. Press.

Finishing

Layer, quilt, and bind your quilt (pages 20–21).

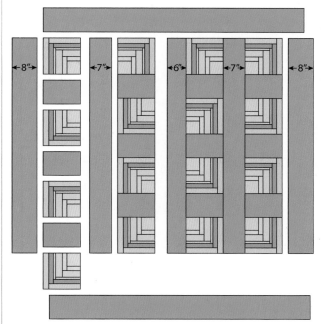

Quilt assembly

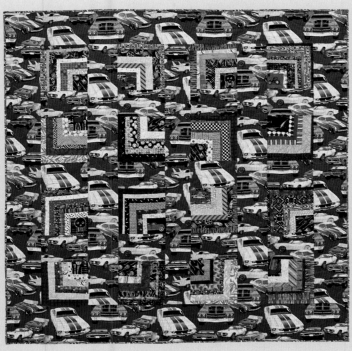

California Cars Housetop, made by Alethea Ballard

This quilt design takes on a whole new personality with each large-image fabric. I paired the jumbo cars with fabrics that included wheels, tools, tractors, fire engines, flames, skulls, and sport fabrics! When people see quilts like this, they really get excited that such wild and crazy images can end up in a quilt. How cool would it be to give this quilt to a special person in your life?

Square Dinkum Poppy, made by Alethea Ballard, machine quilted by Elaine Beatty

square dinkum

Square Dinkum? I spent my elementary school years in a small town in New Zealand. Of course, I learned a whole new way of speaking. Good-Thanks-Ta means thank you, and Crikey Dick means damn it. (Something I wanted to say a lot. Such a naughty girl, even back then!) In Kiwi, the dialect of English unique to New Zealand, "Fair Dinkum" is a phrase that means, in essence, things are pretty good. Someone asks you how you are doing, and you answer, "Ahh, fair dinkum." It actually comes out sounding like, Aaah, feya dyinkum?" (The phrases always end with a question mark as if one is not actually sure of things at all.) That is how this quilt got its name—these are pretty good squares.

Starting with a border fabric is a great way to begin collecting fabrics and colors for a quilt. In each of these Square Dinkum quilts, I found the medium-scale print border fabric first and chose each block's fabric to represent one or two colors present in the border fabric. I made sure that each fabric was rich in color and varied in style.

Choosing fabrics that have a great variety in value is one element that makes this quilt look so fresh and exciting. I selected fabrics ranging from the lightest lights to very dark and dense, thereby taking the quilt from the medium range and giving it a delightful depth and richness.

materials

vibrant lights, mediums, and darks for the blocks

- ¼-yard pieces of 25 different fabrics in a variety of values, scales, and patterns

light, medium, or dark for the pieced inner borders

- ¼ yard, plus the leftovers from cutting the blocks

medium-scale lengthwise-directional print for the setting triangles and outer border

- 2¼ yards

binding

- ⅝ yard

backing

- 3¾ yards

batting

- 64″ × 69″

cutting

vibrant lights, mediums, and darks

- Cut each of the 25 fabrics into 2 strips 2″ × width of fabric for the blocks.

Subcut each paired set of matching strips as follows:

 Cut 1 strip into 6 pieces 2″ × 4½″.

 Cut the remaining strip into 8 pieces 2″ × 5″.

Remove the selvage and trim the leftover pieces to 1½″ wide for the inner border.

light, medium, or dark

- Cut 5 strips 1½″ × width of fabric.

Subcut into random lengths 3–5″ long, for inner border.

medium-scale print

- Cut 2 strips 8¼″ × width of fabric.

Subcut the strips into a total of 7 squares 8¼″ × 8¼″; cut the squares diagonally in both directions for the side setting triangles.

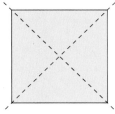

Cut twice diagonally.

Cut 2 squares 4¾″ × 4¾″ from the leftover strips; cut the squares diagonally in one direction for the corner setting triangles.

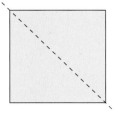

Cut once diagonally.

- Trim the selvage from the remaining fabric and cut 2 strips lengthwise 6½″ × length of fabric for the side borders.

- Cut the following strips crosswise from the remaining fabric:

 Cut 3 identical strips 4″ × remaining width of fabric for the top border.

 Join the strips to make a long continuous strip of fabric (see Making Fabric Wider [or Longer], page 9).

 Cut 3 identical strips 8″ × remaining width of fabric for the bottom border. Join the strips to make a long continuous strip of fabric.

binding

- Cut 7 strips 2½″ × width of fabric.

Use those medium-scale prints! With all of the medium-scale prints available, you have so much to choose from. When designing a quilt with these fabrics, keep in mind the following:

■ When viewed, quilts with medium-scale print fabrics dominating the project seem more subtle and understated.

■ If you plan to use a medium-scale print for the border, small-print fabrics are a natural choice for the inner blocks in a quilt.

■ When working with blocks as small as in this quilt, you can use many fabric bits and scraps to achieve brilliant results.

Bet you can't make just one!

Blocks

Use ¼" seam allowances unless otherwise noted.

1. Arrange the block fabrics into 50 unique sets. Pair the block centers with contrasting frame fabrics, trying to avoid matching up similar values, scale, and patterns. Each set will contain the following:

  1 piece 2" × 4½" for the block centers

  2 pieces 2" × 4½" and 4 pieces 2" × 5" contrasting fabric for the block frame

2. Sew a contrasting 2" × 4½" frame strip to each long side of its corresponding 2" × 4½" block center strip. Press.

3. Trim the strip set into 2 pieces 2" wide.

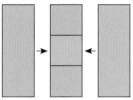

2"   2"

Subcut into 2" units.

4. Sew the matching 2" × 5" frame strips to each side of each of the 2 units. Press.

Add side frame strips.

5. Repeat steps to make 100 blocks 5" × 5".

note

You only need 98 blocks to complete this quilt. The 2 extra blocks can be used as design alternates when assembling the quilt top.

Quilt Assembly

1. Lay out all the blocks and setting triangles on a design surface, following the quilt assembly diagram (page 39). Rotate each block so the seams don't match.

Rotate blocks to alternate seams.

2. Sew the blocks and setting triangles into diagonal rows. Press alternating seams.

3. Trim off the excess setting triangles that stick out at the end of each row.

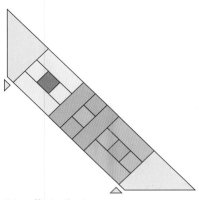

Trim off triangle tips.

4. Sew the rows together. Press.

5. Sew on the corner setting triangles and press the quilt top.

Borders

For more detailed information about adding borders, see Measure, Pin, and Sew, page 19.

Inner Border

1. Sew together randomly cut 1½" inner border strips with the 1½" block leftovers to make 2 top/bottom inner borders that each measure 48" long. Repeat to make 2 side borders that each measure 54" long. Press.

2. Measure vertically through the center of the quilt top and cut the 2 side inner borders to that length.

3. Sew the side inner borders to the quilt. Press.

4. Measure horizontally through the center of the quilt top and cut the top and bottom inner borders to that length.

5. Sew to the top and bottom of the quilt. Press.

Outer Border

1. Measure horizontally through the center of the quilt top and cut the 4" top outer border and the 8" bottom outer border to that length.

2. Sew to the top and bottom of the quilt. Press.

3. Measure vertically through the center of the quilt top and trim the 6½" side outer borders to that length.

4. Sew to the sides of the quilt. Press.

Finishing

Layer, quilt, and bind your quilt (pages 20–21).

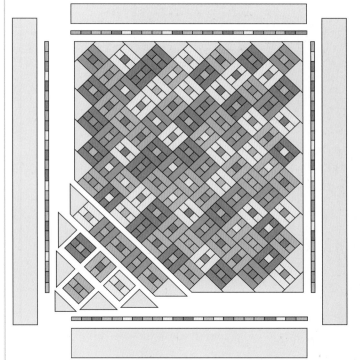

Quilt assembly

Square Dinkum Kitties, made by Alethea Ballard

Finished block: 3⅜″ × 3⅜″   Finished quilt: 36½″ × 38½″

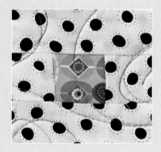

This might just be the cutest baby quilt of the year. With only 50 blocks, the quilt goes together quickly and makes playful use of the small-print fabrics. Cut the block fabric strips to 1⅝″ to make the 3⅜″ blocks. Cut the side borders at 6″ and the top/bottom borders at 4½″. The single fabric in the border that changes from light to dark looks more complicated than it is and is a great way to get movement in the border of the quilt. This is the perfect quilt to show off the medium-scale border prints.

Lily Patch Boxes, made by Alethea Ballard

bella boxes

The two Bella Boxes quilts (*Lily Patch Boxes*, shown above, and *Owl Patch Boxes*, page 44) are actually made from the same stripe fabric but a different alternate fabric for each. Interestingly, the finished results look quite different based on where the stripe fabric is cut. One set of box blocks made from the triangles came out mostly purple and went well with the owl fabric in *Owl Patch Boxes*. The rest of the box blocks ended up quite green and were a great companion to the great Jane Sassaman lily pad fabric that I used in *Lily Patch Boxes*. Using the stripe in the inner border adds a third visual element to the quilt. This design uses just two fabrics, yet it looks more complicated because the stripes are cut so cleverly.

Sometimes simplicity is sublime. For fabric freaks, the idea of using *just* two fabrics in a quilt seems very weird. Yet, stripes can do so much for a quilt, depending on the different ways they are cut and sewn. This quilt is definitely worth a try. Stripes that have varied widths and fewer repeats yield a greater variety of box blocks.

Making little box blocks from stripes is fairly simple and really satisfying. Sew four identically cut triangles together and the box looks pure and solid. Piecing triangles together with stripes that don't align perfectly creates a different look each time and is more funky. Whenever the viewer's eye scans across the fabric looking for matching

materials

medium- to large-motif lengthwise-directional print for alternate blocks and outer border

- 1 yard

stripe that runs parallel to the selvage edges for blocks and inner border

- 1¼ yards

binding

- ⅜ yard

backing

- 1 yard

batting

- 32" × 38"

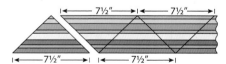

use that fabric: *stripes!*

Use those colorful stripes! Stripes can be cut and sewn back together to make the most wonderful box shapes. Try one stripe or a combination of many. These box blocks are super-cool and can really add a lot of interest to a quilt.

cutting

medium- to large-motif print

- Remove the selvage edge from one side and cut 2 lengthwise strips 4" × length of fabric for the side outer borders.

- Cut the following strips crosswise from the remaining fabric:

  Cut 2 strips 6½" × remaining width of fabric.

  Subcut into a total of 6 squares 6½" × 6½" for the alternate blocks.

- Cut 2 strips 4" × remaining width of fabric for the top and bottom outer borders.

- Cut 4 squares 2" × 2" for the inner border corners.

stripe

- Cut 3 lengthwise strips 3¾" wide parallel to the stripes for the large box blocks. (Most stripes run parallel to the selvage, but check before you cut.)

Subcut 2 sets of 4 matching triangles from each strip (8 total from each strip). The base (long side) will be 7½". Follow the Tip (at right) for cutting quarter-square triangles or use a setting triangle ruler if you have one.

- Cut 1 lengthwise strip 2½" wide parallel to the stripes for the small box blocks.

Subcut 4 sets of 4 matching triangles from the strip (16 total from the strip.) The base (long side) will be 5". Follow the Tip (at right) for cutting quarter-square triangles, but measure 5" along the fabric edge before cutting. If you can't squeeze the sixteenth triangle out of the strip, make one from the leftovers of the larger triangles.

- Cut the following strips crosswise from the remaining fabric:

  Cut 4 crosswise strips 2" × remaining width of fabric for the inner borders.

binding

- Cut 4 strips 2½" × width of fabric.

tip

Here's an easy way to cut quarter-square triangles for 6" squares using long strips of fabric.

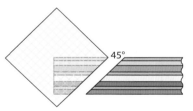

Place ruler's 45° line on top edge of fabric strip and cut along edge.

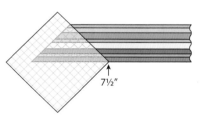

Place ruler's 45° line on bottom edge of fabric strip, measure 7½" from cut edge, and cut along ruler's edge.

Place ruler's 45° line on top edge of fabric strip, measure 7½" from cut edge, and cut along ruler's edge. Cut remaining triangles, alternating measurements along top and bottom edges.

Blocks

Use ¼" seam allowances unless otherwise noted.

1. For each of the 6 large box blocks and each of the 4 small box blocks, match up 2 pairs of triangles and sew them together, starting at the 90° corner and ending on the center point. Take care to push the fabric under the feed dogs, rather than letting the bias edge pull and stretch.

2. Press each seam in the same direction.

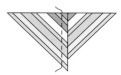

Press seam either left or right, going in the same direction for every seam.

3. Pair the block halves, nesting the seams, and sew them together. Press the center seams open.

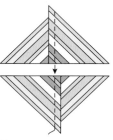

Nest seams.

Press center seam open.

4. Trim off the triangle tips and square the blocks if needed. Make 6 blocks 6½" × 6½" and 4 blocks 4" × 4".

Quilt Assembly

1. Lay out all the blocks on a design surface, following the quilt assembly diagram (page 44) and alternating the large box blocks and alternate blocks.

2. Lace the rows together (page 16).

3. Press the seams towards the alternate blocks.

4. Sew the rows together. Press.

Borders

For more detailed information about adding borders, see Measure, Pin, and Sew, page 19.

Inner Border

1. Measure vertically through the center of the quilt top and cut the 2 side inner borders to that length.

2. Measure horizontally through the center of the quilt top and cut the top and bottom inner borders to that length.

3. Sew the side inner borders to the quilt. Press.

4. Sew an inner border corner to each end of the top and bottom strips. Press.

5. Sew the top and bottom inner borders to the quilt top. Press.

Outer Border

Repeat the instructions for inner borders (above) to add the outer borders, using the small box blocks as the corners. Press and trim to square up, if necessary.

Finishing

Layer, quilt, and bind your quilt (pages 20–21).

Quilt assembly

Owl Patch Boxes, made by Alethea Ballard

These little owls really called out to be featured in a small quilt. They were so cute, I wanted to show them off. By using the lengthwise cutting technique for the side borders, I kept the direction of the fabric correct so the owls didn't end up lying sideways. You will find this cutting technique in many of the quilts in this book. What fun!

Hula Superstars, made by Alethea Ballard

superstars

This just might be one of the brightest, most cheerful quilts I've ever made. These hula girls practically jumped off the shelf and into my arms at a quilt show. I ran around snapping up all the Hawaiian fabrics in the booth and was on my way to making a delightful quilt

The Superstars quilt has many traditional quilt elements. It has a star motif and conventional borders and block layout. Yet it really looks new and fresh when made with modern fabrics. It is a great way to put the spotlight on a collection of fabrics that evoke a clear theme. Using

Choose the fabrics for the star points carefully. They are the unifying element in the design. Use contrasting colors for the triangles surrounding the blocks' centers. After that you can play with the centers; the quilt will really show off a fun collection of fabrics!

materials

light #1 for Four-Patch blocks and prairie-point units

■ ½ yard

light #2 for Six-Patch blocks and prairie-point units

■ ½ yard

medium light for quarter-square triangle blocks (B)

■ ⅝ yard

medium #1 for Four-Patch, Six-Patch, and Nine-Patch blocks

■ ½ yard total of a variety of fabrics or scraps

medium #2 for quarter-square triangle blocks (C)

■ ⅝ yard

medium dark for folded inner border strip (optional)

■ ⅓ yard

dark #1 for prairie-point triangles

■ ⅜ yard

dark #2 for quarter-square triangle blocks (A)

■ ¾ yard

dark #3 for inner border

■ ½ yard

novelty lengthwise-directional print for outer borders and centers

■ 1⅞ yards

binding

■ ⅝ yard

backing

■ 3¼ yards

batting

■ 57″ × 75″

cutting

light #1

■ Cut 2 strips 3½″ × width of fabric.

Subcut the strips to make the following:

8 squares 3½″ × 3½″ for the Four-Patch blocks

6 rectangles 3½″ × 6½″ for the prairie-point units

light #2

■ Cut 3 strips 3½″ × width of fabric.

Subcut the strips to make the following:

12 squares 3½″ × 3½″ for the Six-Patch blocks

8 rectangles 3½″ × 6½″ for the prairie-point units

medium light

■ Cut 2 strips 7½″ × width of fabric.

Subcut into a total of 6 squares 7½″ × 7½″ for the star quarter-square triangles (B).

medium #1

■ Cut 3 strips 3½″ × width of fabric.

Subcut into a total of 28 squares 3½″ × 3½″ for the Four-Patch, Six-Patch, and Nine-Patch blocks.

medium #2

■ Cut 2 strips 7½″ × width of fabric.

Subcut into a total of 6 squares 7½″ × 7½″ for the inner quarter-square triangles (C).

medium dark

■ Cut 5 strips 1″ × width of fabric for the folded inner border strips (optional).

dark #1

■ Cut 2 strips 4½″ × width of fabric.

Subcut into a total of 14 squares 4½″ × 4½″ for the prairie-point units.

dark #2

■ Cut 3 strips 7½″ × width of fabric.

Subcut 12 squares 7½″ × 7½″ for the quarter-square triangles (A).

dark #3

■ Cut 5 strips 2½″ × width of fabric for the inner border.

novelty print

■ Remove the selvage edges and cut 2 lengthwise strips 7″ × length of fabric for the side borders.

■ Cut the following strips crosswise from the remaining fabric:

Cut 3 identical strips 7″ × remaining width of fabric for the top border. Join the strips to make a long continuous strip of fabric (see Making Fabric Wider [or Longer], page 9).

Cut 3 identical strips 7″ × remaining width of fabric for the bottom border. Join the strips to make a long continuous strip of fabric.

■ Fussy cut 8 squares 6½″ × 6½″ for the block centers.

■ Fussy cut 6 rectangles 3½″ × 6½″ for the Six-Patch blocks.

binding

■ Cut 7 strips 2½″ × width of fabric.

Blocks

Use ¼″ seam allowances unless otherwise noted.

Quarter-square triangle

Four-Patch block

Paired quarter-square triangle

Six-Patch block

Nine-Patch block

use that fabric: *a treasured collection!*

Use that treasured collection. We all know what it's like to collect fabrics in a theme, whether it is cowboys or snowmen, butterflies or roses, or Elvis. There is an element in this process where the collector wants to hold onto the collection, feels it is not complete, wants to keep looking, and certainly doesn't want to use up the fabric in case a better opportunity comes along. Am I right, or what? Well, here is the skinny. With this quilt, all you have to do is use a few 6″ squares and some 3″ squares, and you have a fabulous way to display the collection. Then you can keep on collecting to your heart's content. Come on, you can use a little bitty bit of the collection, can't you? Yes! Do it now!

Prairie-Point Units

1. Fold the 4½″ dark #1 squares in half diagonally, wrong sides together, and press.

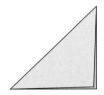

Fold diagonally and press.

2. Fold them in half again diagonally and press. Repeat Steps 1–2 to make 14 prairie points.

Make 14.

3. Press the 3½″ × 6½″ light #1 and light #2 rectangles in half vertically to make a fold line down the center.

4. Align a prairie point on the fold line, with the raw edges even with one long side of the rectangle. Baste the prairie point to the edge using long stitches and a scant ¼″ seam allowance.

5. Repeat Steps 3–4 to make a total of 14 prairie-point units (6 of light #1 fabric and 8 of light #2 fabric).

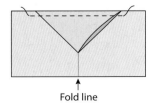

Fold line

Make 14.

tip ·

Using tangible triangles—One way to add a triangle shape, as well as a dimensional element, to a quilt is to insert a prairie point into the seam, rather than piecing the triangle. A prairie point is a square of fabric folded twice on a diagonal that results in a folded triangle point with all the raw edges stacked on top of each other, ready to be sewn into a seam. Prairie points are a great way to add visual interest, and using them removes the need to make the mathematical calculations to figure out how to piece that triangle into that block. Super tricky!

Quarter-Square Triangle Units

1. Draw a diagonal center line, on the wrong side, across 12 dark #2 (A) 7½″ squares.

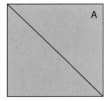

Draw diagonal line on wrong side of square (A).

2. Place a square (A) on each of the 6 medium-light squares (B), right sides together. Then place a square (A) on each of the 6 medium #2 squares (C), right sides together.

3. Sew ¼″ seams on each side of the diagonal line for all 12 paired squares; then cut along the center line.

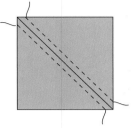

Sew ¼″ on each side of line.

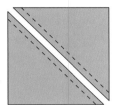

Cut along center line.

4. Press the seams toward (A) to create 24 half-square triangles (12 A/B units and 12 A/C units).

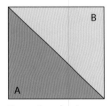 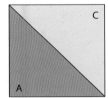

Press pieced units open.

5. Pair the 12 A/B units with the 12 A/C units. Stack the pairs, right sides facing, nesting the seams tightly with the A fabrics opposite each other along the seams. Pin to secure the seams in place, keeping the pins clear from the center of the square.

6. Draw a new diagonal center line, crossing through the seam.

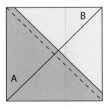

Draw new diagonal line.

7. Sew ¼″ on each side of the center line for all 12 paired squares; then cut along the center line.

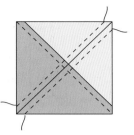

Sew ¼″ on each side of line.

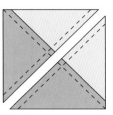

Cut along new center line.

8. Press the seams open to create 24 quarter-square triangle blocks.

9. Trim the blocks to 6½″ × 6½″.

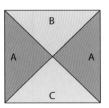

Make 24.

tip . . . .

When squaring up a 6½″ quarter-square or half-square block, it is really helpful to use a 6½″-square ruler with a diagonal line, but a 6½″ × 12½″ ruler with a diagonal line will work fine too. Place the diagonal line along the center seam and trim one side and the top. Turn the block and align the diagonal line along the center seam. Trim the remaining side and top.

Paired Quarter-Square Triangle Units

1. Pin and sew 14 quarter-square triangles into 7 paired units, matching (B) fabrics along the seam.

2. Press the seam open.

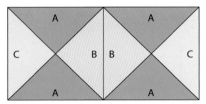

Make 7.

Maverick Quilter Says

I can't live without my design wall. I learn everything I need to know about my work from looking at it on my design wall. I see what is working and what is not. I can see if fabrics are dulling the colors or if the borders are too big/small/boring and so on. I usually sew 2 blocks at a time and constantly add to the design wall and move things around. This is my chance to touch the beautiful fabrics and see how the work is coming together. I need to see how things are going before I sew the blocks together. I move things around until it all "clicks," and then I know it's ready to sew together. Sometimes a project stays on the wall a long time before it clicks, but even a quilt maverick can be patient.

Four-Patch Blocks

1. Lay out 3½" squares, following the four-patch assembly diagram, using 2 medium #1 squares and 2 light #1 squares.

2. Chain sew (page 14) to join the squares.

3. Press toward the darker fabrics.

4. Nest the seams and chain sew to assemble the Four-Patch blocks. Press.

5. Repeat Steps 1–4 to make 4 blocks.

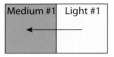

Four-patch assembly—make 4.

Six-Patch Blocks

1. Lay out the block following the six-patch assembly diagram, using 2 medium #1 squares, 2 light #2 squares, 1 light #1 prairie-point unit, and 1 fussy-cut 3½" × 6½" novelty print.

2. Chain sew to join the pieces.

3. Press the seams away from the prairie points.

4. Nest the seams, pin, and chain sew to assemble the blocks. Press.

5. Repeat Steps 1–4 to make 6 blocks.

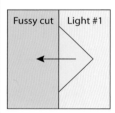

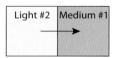

Six-patch assembly—make 6.

Nine-Patch Blocks

1. Lay out 1 novelty print 6½" × 6½" block center with 4 light #2 prairie-point units and 4 medium #1 squares, following the nine-patch assembly diagram

2. Lace the rows together (page 16).

3. Press the seams away from the prairie points.

4. Nest the seams and sew the rows together. Press.

5. Repeat Steps 1–4 to make 2 blocks.

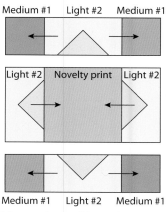

Medium #1   Light #2   Medium #1

Light #2   Novelty print   Light #2

Medium #1   Light #2   Medium #1

Nine-patch assembly—make 2.

Quilt Assembly

1. Lay out all the blocks on a design surface, following the photo (page 47) and the quilt assembly diagram (page 52).

2. Lace the rows together (page 16).

3. Press.

4. Sew the rows together. Press.

Borders

For more detailed information about adding borders, see Measure, Pin, and Sew, page 19.

Folded Inner Border ¼˝ Strips

1. Trim off the selvage edges of the 5 medium dark 1˝ strips.

2. Join 3 of the strips into a long strip, using a small stitch length.

3. Press the seams open.

4. Cut the long strip in half widthwise to make 2 equal-length strips for the side borders.

5. Press the 4 (2 short and 2 long) strips in half lengthwise, wrong sides together, to create ½˝-wide inner border strips.

6. Baste a long folded inner border strip to each side of the quilt top, aligning the raw edges and using a scant ¼˝ seam allowance. Trim off the excess. Repeat with the short inner border strips for the top and bottom edges of the quilt top.

tip

When basting a folded border strip, sew with the back of the quilt top facing you and the folded strip against the feed dogs. This keeps the pieced seams facing you, allowing you to flatten them as you sew. It also keeps the raw edges of the quilt top from stretching (see Making Friends with the Feed Dogs, page 15).

Inner Border

1. Measure horizontally through the center of the quilt top and cut the 2½˝ top and bottom inner border strips to that length.

2. Sew the top and bottom borders to the quilt top. Press.

3. Trim off the selvage edges and join 3 inner border 2½˝ strips into a long strip using a small stitch length. Press the seams open.

4. Measure vertically through the center of the quilt top and cut the 2 side borders to that length.

5. Sew the side borders to the quilt top. Press.

Outer Border

1. Measure vertically through the center of the quilt top and cut the 7˝ side outer border strips to that length.

2. Sew the side borders to the quilt top. Press.

3. Measure horizontally through the center of the quilt top and cut the top and bottom outer borders to that length.

4. Sew the top and bottom outer borders to the quilt top. Press.

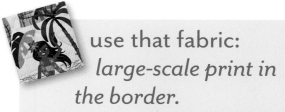

use that fabric:
large-scale print in the border.

Using a large-scale border print creates an exuberant quilt! Try it!

Finishing

Layer, quilt, and bind your quilt (pages 20–21).

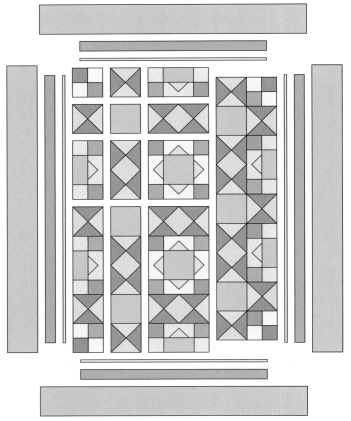

Quilt assembly

Cowboy Superstars, made by Alethea Ballard, machine quilting by Laura Lee Fritz

Cowboy Superstars shows how each novelty print can create a completely different look to this classic design. In this version, each block center and all of the 3½″ squares are a different fabric from a collection of cowboy fabrics. This can be a great project to show off those prized fabrics you have been collecting.

Emerald Jalousie, made by Alethea Ballard, machine quilting by Elaine Beatty

FINISHED BLOCK: Various   **FINISHED QUILT:** 51" × 64"

jalousie

I saw this flowered fabric and thought it was so beautiful that I wanted to see the whole thing. It would have been easy to just put a border around it and call it a day. Then I came up with something so much better.

Right now we are in a fabulous age for fabric. There are so many really large-scale floral prints in such appealing colors. When we are at the fabric store, we all want to use them in our quilts, but how? They are often used on a border or in oversize blocks to showcase the print. Instead of cutting this fabric into chunks and placing the pieces around a quilt, just make the fabric become the quilt itself. This is a great way to showcase spectacular fabric in an innovative way.

Find a fabric that makes your heart vibrate. You know what I mean: you see the fabric and you feel like you just have to have it! Find 8–12

fabrics to use as vertical inset strips that will coordinate with the large-scale background fabric. Choose a different coordinating print for vertical and horizontal sashing that coordinates well with the large-scale background fabric. If possible, pick fabrics from a matching fabric line, selecting fabrics that match one of the individual colors of the large-scale fabric. Augment the selection with some interesting companion fabrics. I chose zucchini, cactus, and marbled fabrics to round out my selections. Be playful and fun; this is a pleasure you are indulging in!

In Jalousie, strips are inserted at random intervals to create a dynamic visual effect. The background stays visually intact, and you have created a masterpiece. If you can sew a straight line, you can make the center of this quilt.

materials

large-scale lengthwise-directional print for quilt center

- 1¾ yards

coordinating prints for inset strips

- ⅛ yard each of 8–12 fabrics or scraps that match one of the individual colors in the large-scale background fabric

print #1 for sashing and inner border

- 1 yard that closely resembles the color of the large-scale print and blends in well

print #2 for outer border

- 1 yard

binding

- ⅝ yard

backing

- 3⅛ yards

batting

- 55" × 68"

cutting

large-scale print

- Remove the selvage edge and cut to exactly 40" × 53" for the quilt center.

coordinating prints

- Cut strips 1" × width of fabric from a variety of fabrics for inset strips. The number of strips needed will vary depending on how the rows are subcut (Step 5, page 57). Cut a few strips to start, and cut more as you need them.

print #1

- Cut 12 strips 1" × width of fabric for the sashing.

- Cut 3 strips 5" × width of fabric for the inner border.

print #2

- Cut 3 strips 8" × width of fabric for the outer border.

binding

- Cut 7 strips 2½" × width of fabric.

tip

Make a practice piece to check your ¼" seams. Cut 2 pieces of fabric the exact same size and exact same motif. Use a rotary cutter to cut several vertical lines through one of the fabric pieces. In the cut piece, use a ¼" seam to sew 1" strips of fabric between each cut edge, joining the piece back together with the inset strips. Press the block flat with the seams open and lay this practice piece next to the intact piece. Both pieces should be the same size.

If the sewn block is narrower, adjust your ¼" marker or foot to sew a slightly smaller seam allowance (maybe only 1 or 2 thread widths). If the sewn block is larger, adjust your ¼" marker or foot to sew a slightly larger seam allowance (maybe only 1 or 2 thread widths). See Alter That Fabric (pages 9–11). Practice until you can make the sewn piece stay exactly the right size.

Both pieces should be the same size after adding the inset strip.

Construction Information

The method of constructing this quilt works from the principle that the two ¼" seam allowances, which are created by each cut you make in the background, are offset by the ½" finished inset strips, which are inserted between the cuts. After all the cutting and sewing, the quilt center should be the same size as the original fabric (40" × 53"). Using this method, you can easily inset any fabric into the background and keep the background visually intact.

Work on one horizontal section (or row) of the quilt at a time. Each row will be cut as you go. Each row in your quilt will be a different height from mine because the cuts are based on the fabric you are using. Avoid cutting through the centers of the flowers; they are key visual elements. Before you start cutting each row, stitch along the *top* of each fabric section about ⅛" from the edge. This is an essential step that lets you keep track of the top edge and helps you put the cut rows back together.

Rows

Use ¼" seam allowances unless otherwise noted.

note

Avoid cutting through major design elements of the fabric, such as flowers or faces. Use these motifs as a guide to determine how many horizontal rows to cut and the width of each block. You may have 5, 6, or 7 rows, depending on your fabric, and the size of the blocks will vary in each row.

1. Use a basting stitch to sew a line ⅛" from the top edge (40") of the large-scale quilt center fabric. This will remind you which edge is the top.

2. Cut a strip, between 3"–8", off the top edge of the quilt center fabric.

3. Cut the row vertically in 4 random places. This creates 5 random-size blocks.

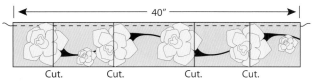

Cut strip into 5 random-size blocks.

4. Cut 4 vertical sashing strips 1″ × the height of the row from print #1. Arrange the 5 blocks on the design surface with a vertical sashing strip placed between each block. Use the basted edge to orient the top edge of the blocks.

tip ....

With the variety of 1″ fabric strips used in this project, keeping all the pieces in order may seem challenging. A quick tip is to remember that all sashing strips are cut from the same fabric—print #1.

5. Subcut the 5 blocks by making 1–4 random vertical cuts through each. Reposition the cut blocks on the design surface.

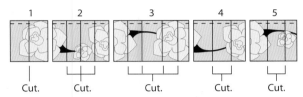

Randomly subcut each block 1–4 times.

6. Trim the 1″ coordinating print inset strips to the height of this row, using a different fabric for each block and cutting only the number of strips as there were subcuts in the blocks. Arrange the cut inset strips on the design surface between each subcut block piece.

7. Using a ¼″ seam, sew the inset strips and vertical sashing between the cut edges of the blocks, rejoining the cut pieces into a continuous row. Keep the fabric orientation correct by making sure the stitched line is along the top edge at all times. Press the seams open. Check that your seams are the right size by comparing them to the uncut quilt center fabric. Remember that you have a little wiggle room with pinning and sewing in which to help the sections match (see Tip, page 55). You must measure and pin borders (page 19).

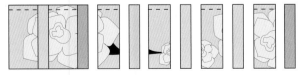

Sew inset and sashing strips to join row.

8. Repeat this process to make several varying-height rows, continuing until the entire quilt center fabric has been cut into rows and the rows have been reassembled with inset and sashing strips (see Note, page 56). Remember to baste the top edge of the quilt center fabric before cutting each vertical strip. To aid in assembling the quilt top, label each row numerically as it is completed.

Quilt Assembly

1. Lay out the rows in the order they were cut from the quilt center fabric. Keep the rows' orientation correct by making sure the stitched line is along the top edge.

2. Measure vertically through the center of the quilt top and trim the 1″ horizontal sashing strips to that length (40″) from print #1. Cut enough strips to insert a strip between each row. (Note: If you have 6 rows, you'll need 5 horizontal sashing strips.)

3. Sew the rows together, inserting a horizontal sashing strip between each row.

4. Press the whole quilt center flat and trim the sides to square it up, if necessary. (Note: If the seam allowance was accurate, the pieced quilt top should measure 40″ × 53″. See Construction Information, page 56.)

Maverick Quilter Says

When your sewing needs to look flat, use a thin sewing thread. The larger the number on the spool, the thinner the thread. A bobbin thread or piecing thread labeled #50 works well and can make the seams lie flatter and recede.

Borders

For more detailed information about adding borders and cutting curved pieces, see Measure, Pin, and Sew, page 19, Creating Curves, page 12, and Goddess block construction, pages 61–63.

1. Remove the selvage edges from the 5″ inner border strips and sew 2 of the pieces into a continuous strip for the side borders. Press the seams open. Repeat for the 8″ outer border strips.

2. Cut the strips to the same length.

3. Refer to Goddess block construction (pages 61–63) for an illustration of wavy piecing. Center a 5″ inner border strip on top of a corresponding 8″ outer border strip, right sides up, aligning the top and bottom edges. Press the strips flat to merge the fabrics as much as possible.

tip . . . .

When cutting the curves, it is important that the stacked strips line up at the top and bottom edges. If the strips are not aligned at the top and bottom during cutting, they will not sew together well.

4. Freehand cut the curves, starting and ending with a short straight section.

5. Pair up opposite curvy strips, right sides facing up.

6. Keep the paired fabrics on top of each other and clip the inner curves horizontally, cutting less than ¼″ deep.

7. Turn one of the curvy strips right side facing down. Align the fabrics along a vertical line on the rotary mat, aligning the top and bottom edges. Use the horizontal lines to help make marks that indicate where the pieces match up. Use a pencil and make little marks on the peaks and valleys of the curves.

8. Pin 2 paired strips together at each peak and valley. This will look unwieldy, but things will work out when the pieces are sewn together.

9. Sew the paired strips together with a ¼″ seam, backstitching at the beginning and end. Gently push or pull the fabrics horizontally to keep the part under the needle overlapping evenly. Do not pull or stretch the fabric vertically, since it will stretch the fabrics and cause problems.

tip . . . .

A stiletto (like Alex Anderson's 4-in-1 Essential Sewing Tool, C&T Publishing) is useful to pull the bottom layer of fabric into place and hold the pieces together as you guide them under the foot.

10. Press from the back first, laying the seam flat to one side. Turn over and press from the front. Allow the fabric to cool in place to set the seam and help it lie flat.

11. Repeat the curvy piecing to make all 4 borders. Trim all borders to 6″ wide.

12. Measure horizontally through the center of the quilt top and cut the shorter curvy-pieced top and bottom borders to that length (40″).

13. Pin and sew the top and bottom borders to the quilt top. Press.

14. Measure vertically through the center of the quilt top and cut the long curvy-pieced side borders to that length.

15. Pin and sew the side borders to the quilt. Press.

Finishing

Layer, quilt, and bind your quilt (pages 20–21).

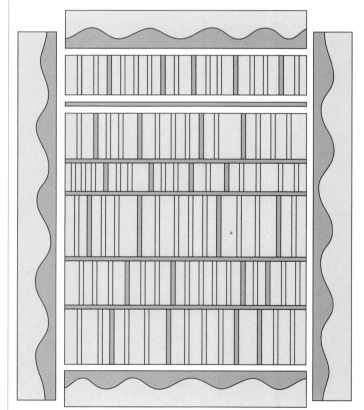

Quilt assembly

Maverick Quilter Says

One of the pitfalls of being a fabric nut is that we occasionally give in to a purchasing impulse that, upon reflection, was a mediocre choice. I have 6 yards of weird bunny fabric in two colors that could make some cute baby quilts, but the truth is that I don't want to touch it. I have moved on and am so over that bunny fabric. A maverick has to bite the bullet, cut her losses, and get rid of the dang thing. It is taking up space in the stash, and when you're honest with yourself, you know you'll never use it. Ever.

The best way to alleviate your "I paid $60 for this fabric" guilt is to find a worthy cause and donate the fabric. If you loved it once, it must be nice, and someone else will love it too, someday. With all the charitable work being done, you have to just pick a cause; someone is making quilts for those people. Your fabrics can go to make pillowcases for children with life-changing illnesses, quilts for soldiers, and comfort objects for people in need. Usually it is also a tax write-off, so reduce the guilt and give it away! These are my favorite charities:

- ConKerr Cancer—A Case for Smiles
  www.conkerrcancer.org

- Quilts of Valor Foundation
  www.QOVF.org

- Linus Foundation
  www.linusfoundation.org

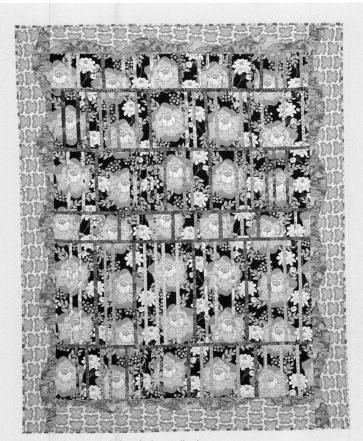

Ginger Jalousie, made by Alethea Ballard

I came across this gorgeous ginger flower fabric, and I had that "just have to have it" response. It is so gratifying to work my way down this quilt and see all the ways the background can interact with the different inset strip and sashing colors. A jalousie is louvered glass window used in hot climates. I like the idea of parallel lines dividing the "view," yet allowing most if it to show through. Love it!

Goddess Flowers, made by Alethea Ballard

goddess

This quilt is really fun to make, since each fabric pairing gives such different and interesting results. Each cut is also unique, resulting in a new look each time. Sewing these curvy blocks becomes like a birthday party, where you unwrap each present and delight in the surprise revealed.

Select fabrics with the idea that you'll pair each fabric with two others. Vary them from dark to light to give the design depth and variety. The sashing fabric makes a big impact, and it might need to be selected after the blocks are finished to get the right balance of color and pattern.

While the curves may seem daunting, it is easy to master them, and they give you so many possibilities. This is a great project for unleashing your creative self. The blocks are made a little oversize, and you can vary the widths as you put the blocks together. It is also really easy to make this quilt another size by changing the number of curvy blocks you use. So dig in!

materials

dark mediums, mediums, and lights for curvy blocks
- ½ yard each of 10 different fabrics

medium for sashing and inner border
- 1½ yards

medium dark for outer border
- 1⅝ yards

binding
- ¾ yard

backing
- 5 yards

batting
- 85" × 85"

cutting

dark mediums, mediums, and lights

From each of the 10 fabrics, cut as follows for the curvy blocks:

- Cut 1 strip 7" × width of fabric. Trim the selvage edges.

Subcut the strip into 2 pieces 7" × 20".

- Cut 1 strip 5" × width of fabric.

Subcut the strip into 2 pieces 5" × 20".

medium

- Cut 7 strips 4" × width of fabric.

Subcut 3 of the strips to total 6 pieces 4" × 19½" for the horizontal sashing. Keep the 4 remaining strips for the vertical sashing.

- Cut 8 strips 2½" × width of fabric for the inner border.

medium dark

- Cut 8 strips 6½" × width of fabric for the outer border.

binding

- Cut 9 strips 2½" × width of fabric.

Blocks

Use ¼" seam allowances unless otherwise noted. For more detailed information about cutting curved pieces, see Creating Curves, page 12.

1. Arrange the 5" and 7" curvy block strips into 20 paired sets containing a strip of each width. For each set, select fabrics that have contrast and will add variety to the finished blocks.

2. Center a 5" strip on top of its paired 7" strip, matching the strips at the top and bottom edges, with right sides facing up.

3. Use a smooth motion to free cut a gentle curve through the center of the 2 strips, starting and ending with a short straight section.

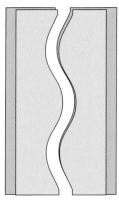

Cut gentle curves, starting and ending with short straight sections.

4. Pair up opposite curvy strips, right sides facing up.

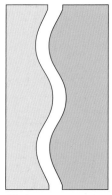

Clip inner curves using a scant ¼" cut.

5. Keep the fabrics paired and clip the inner curves horizontally, cutting less than ¼" deep.

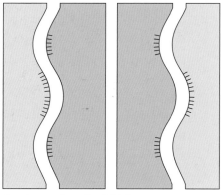

Match opposite pairs of fabrics.

6. Turn one of the curvy strips right side facing down. Align the fabrics along a vertical line on the rotary mat, aligning the top and bottom edges. Use the horizontal lines to make marks that indicate where the pieces match up. Using a pencil, make little marks on the peaks and valleys of the curves.

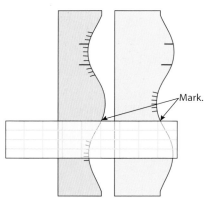

Mark.

Draw matching marks on peaks and valleys.

7. Pin the paired strips together at each marked peak and valley, right sides together. This will look unwieldy, but things will work out when the pieces are sewn together.

8. Sew the paired strips together with a ¼" seam, back-stitching at the beginning and end. Gently push or pull the fabrics horizontally to keep the parts under the needle overlapping evenly. Do not pull or stretch the fabric vertically, since stretching the fabrics will cause problems. A stiletto (see Tip, page 58) is useful to pull the underneath fabric into place and hold the pieces together as you guide them under the foot.

9. Press from the back first, laying the seam flat to one side. Turn it over and press from the front. Allow it to cool in place to set the seam and help it lie flat.

10. Trim the curve-pieced strip to measure 5¼" × 19½".

11. Repeat the curvy cuts and piecing to make 40 curve-pieced strips.

Maverick Quilter Says

If you have never sewn curves before, now is the time. It is easier than it looks, and the results are so exciting. If you go slowly and start with gentle curves, you can progress to more dramatic shapes quickly. I had to take out some seams when I started, but the pinning and marking that I do now really helps. If you find yourself way off in the middle of a block, stop. Have a cup of tea, remove the stitching, and start over. No worries.

12. Arrange the curve-pieced strips into 9 blocks of 4 strips each. There are 4 extra curve-pieced strips, so lay out all the curvy strips and move them around until you are pleased with the layout.

13. Sew 4 curve-pieced strips together, along the long edges, to create each block. Press and trim each block to measure 19½″ × 19½″.

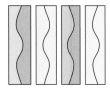

Block assembly

tip . . . .

Use a permanent pen to number nine flower-head pins. Once you have the desired layout of your quilt assembly, label the quilt blocks using the numbered flower-head pins. Put the pins in the same position in each block (the upper left corner); then you will get the correct block with the correct orientation when adding the sashings.

Use numbered flower-head pins for markers.

Quilt Assembly

1. Lay out all the blocks and horizontal sashing on a design surface, following the quilt assembly diagram (page 64).

2. Sew the blocks and horizontal sashing into vertical rows.

3. Press the seams toward the sashing.

4. Measure the rows and trim them to the same length.

5. Join the 2 vertical sashing strips into a long strip using a small stitch length. Press the seams open. Repeat with the 2 remaining strips to create 2 vertical sashing strips.

6. Trim the strips to match the length of the rows. Pin and sew the vertical sashing strips to join the rows.

7. Press and trim to square up the quilt center.

Borders

For more detailed information about adding borders, see Measure, Pin, and Sew, page 19.

Inner Border

1. Trim off the selvage edges of 2 of the 2½″ inner border strips and join them into a long strip using a small stitch length. Press the seams open. Repeat to make another side inner border strip.

2. Measure vertically through the center of the quilt top and trim the side inner border strips to this length.

3. Sew the side inner borders to the quilt top. Press.

4. Repeat Steps 1–3 to make and add the top and bottom inner borders.

Outer Border

Repeat the instructions above for inner borders to add the outer borders. Press and trim to square up, if necessary.

Finishing

Layer, quilt, and bind your quilt (pages 20–21).

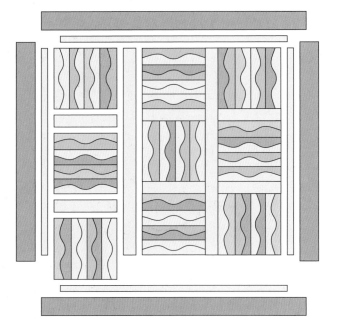

Quilt assembly

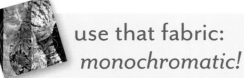

use that fabric: *monochromatic!*

Using fabrics from a single color can give very pleasing results. Within a color there are different tints, tones, and hues, depending on the amount of white, black, or other colors in the dye. Finding the right matching yellow for a project can be tricky, but using lots of yellows together can really sing. As always, I advise you to include some playful fabrics. It's fun to sneak in some funny fabrics in a monochromatic quilt.

A little dab of complementary color here and there is another trick to really make the quilt look artistic and to help a monochromatic scheme seem vibrant. Red or orange with green, or yellow with purple or blue are great combinations.

Green Goddess, made by Alethea Ballard

Finished quilt: 46¼″ × 53¾″

This was the original Goddess quilt, and I made it for my friends as a wedding quilt. Working without a plan (as usual), I was surprised and delighted to see the feminine, earthy shapes unfolding as I created them. Instead of making pieced blocks, I randomly joined pieced strips to make the quilt center and separated the rows with horizontal sashing. I added complementary color shapes to some of the blocks for a punch of color. Using a monochromatic theme allowed me to use unexpected fabrics like zucchini, cactus, and dandelion weeds. I really love using fabrics that surprise you when you look closely.

Flowered Dishes, made by Alethea Ballard

dishes

Dishes is another fabric-lover's delight. It has large spaces that can accommodate large images or appliqué. The visual interplay of the patterns, colors, and fabrics creates a dramatic effect and is exciting to look at.

Putting the curved pieces together is a delightful way to play with big flowers and bright colors. The crosses in the centers serve both as a frame and a visual balance. They create repetition and give the design structure. Bright or bold colors will really stand out, while quieter colors will recede. Whatever fabric theme you use, the results are exciting, surprising, and satisfying.

The construction of this quilt is a little tricky and requires some experience. That said, when you do have all the fussy curve-pieced blocks made, the top goes together fast. With no borders—just 13 blocks and the setting triangles—you can put it together quickly, and you're off to quilting.

materials

flower print for convex (A) pieces

- 2+ yards total of a variety of fabrics or 36 pieces 7″ × 7″ (Note: Extra fabric is allotted for fussy cutting flower motifs.)

contrasting fabrics for concave (B) pieces and leaves (C)

- 1¾ yards total of a variety of fabrics or 36 pieces 7″ × 7″ (Note: I cut the leaves using leftovers from the concave pieces.)

solids for the block crosses

- ⅓ yard each of 3 different fabrics— Choose fabrics with good contrast to the curve blocks.

neutral or large motif for alternate blocks

- ⅞ yard, or more if the large motif needs fussy cutting

medium-size motif print for alternate-block triangles

- ⅓ yard

medium- or small-motif print for side setting triangle corners

- ⅓ yard

large-motif print for setting triangles

- 1 yard

binding

- ½ yard

backing

- 3 yards

batting

- 53″ × 53″

template plastic

fusible web

---

cutting

flower print

- Cut 36 convex (A) pieces (see Drunkard's Path units, page 67)

contrasting fabrics

- Cut 36 concave (B) pieces (see Drunkard's Path units, page 67)

- Cut 12 leaves from leftover concave pieces (*optional*: see Alternate Blocks, page 69)

solids

- Cut 1 strip 4¾″ × width of fabric from each of the 3 fabrics.

Subcut the strip into 3 strips 4½″ × 13″ for the cross bars.

- Cut 2 strips 1½″ × width of fabric from each of the 3 fabrics.

Subcut the strips into a total of 4 strips 1½″ × 13″ for the cross ends and centers.

neutral or large motif

- Fussy cut 4 rectangles 8⅞″ × 16¾″ for the alternate blocks.

medium-size motif print

- Cut 4 squares 6¼″ × 6¼″.

Subcut each square in half diagonally for the alternate block triangles.

medium- or small-motif print

- Cut 4 squares 5½″ × 5½″.

Subcut each square in half diagonally for the border setting triangle.

large-motif fabric

- Cut 2 squares 9¾″ × 9¾″.

Subcut each square in half diagonally for the corner triangles.

- Cut 3 strips 5½″ × width of fabric for the border setting polygon.

binding

- Cut 6 strips 2½″ × width of fabric.

---

tip

Try a couple of practice Drunkard's Path blocks to get your rhythm and to work out any issues. It also helps you see how the fabrics are looking together, so you can make changes before you get too far into the project.

use that fabric: *large florals*

Cutting large florals off-centered and pairing them up leads to such wonderful visual treats

Blocks

Use ¼" seam allowances unless otherwise noted.

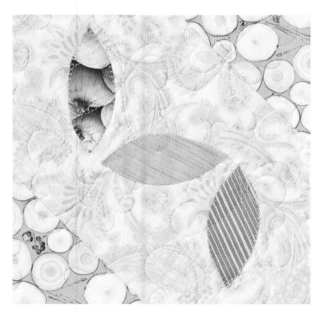

Drunkard's Path Units

Each Drunkard's Path unit consists of a convex (A) and a concave (B) piece. You will need 36 blocks.

1. Trace template patterns (A), (B), and optional (C) (page 71) onto template plastic. Mark the ¼" seam allowances and grainlines on the templates to help cut the pieces and accurately sew them together. Cut out the plastic templates.

2. Trace 36 templates (A) and (B) onto the right side of the corresponding fabrics. Position the corners of the templates on the grainlines so that the curves will be on the bias, giving you the flexibility needed to sew the curve. Position and trace template (A) on the fabric so that the flower designs are well within the ¼" seam allowance. Draw around the template with a pencil, then rotary cut the straight corners, and use scissors to cut the curves.

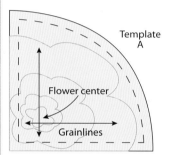

Cut convex (A) pieces with flower centers inside the ¼" seam allowance.

3. Arrange the convex (A) and concave (B) pieces into 36 paired sets. Pair fabrics to provide a pleasing arrangement of values and contrast in the block design.

4. Clip the (B) pieces along the seam allowance, beginning and ending about 1" from the edges. Make the clips less than ¼" deep and about ¼" apart. Careful clipping in the seam on the concave side of the block will help make the sewing successful.

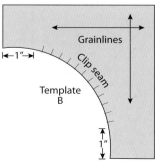

Clip concave seam allowance a scant ¼" deep and ¼" apart.

5. Fold both pieces in half, aligning the straight edges, and finger-press the curved edge at the fold to mark the middle.

6. Place concave piece (B) onto its corresponding convex piece (A), right sides together, and pin the center.

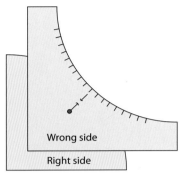

Pin center of curve.

7. Pin the rest of the seam.

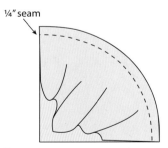

Pin seam.

8. Sew the seam. Use a stiletto to keep the edges of the seams even.

¼" seam

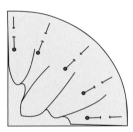

Sew seam.

9. Press the seam gently toward (B).

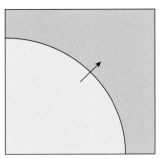

Press toward (B).

10. Trim to 5½" × 5½", if necessary. Make 36.

Cross Units

Arrange the cross block fabrics into 3 sets. Each set will contain 3 strips 4½" × 13" for bars, 3 strips 1½" × 13" for ends, and 1 strip 1½" × 13" for the center. Label the sets Cross #1, Cross #2, and Cross #3. Work with one set of fabrics at a time, starting with Cross #1.

1. Sew 1 end strip 1½" × 13" to each 4½" × 13" bar strip to make 3 strip sets. Press.

2. Cut 1 strip set into 8 pieces 1½" wide for the single-post units.

1½"

Cut single-post units.

3. Sew the remaining 2 strip sets to each long side of the 1½" × 13" center strip to make a double-post strip set. Press.

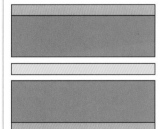

Make double-post strip set.

4. Cut the double-post strip set into 4 pieces 1½" wide for the double-post units.

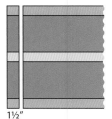

1½"

Cut double-post units.

5. At this point there are 4 double-post units and 8 single-post units from Cross #1. This is enough to make 4 matching Cross blocks. Repeat Steps 1–4 with the remaining sets of fabrics to make the following:

Cross #2: Make 6 single-post units and 3 double-post units for 3 matching cross blocks.

Cross #3: Make 4 single-post units and 2 double-post units for 2 matching cross blocks.

Maverick Quilter Says

Each block needs 1 double-post unit and 2 single-post units to make the cross units. For *Flowered Dishes* (page 65), I made 4 sets of crosses in blue, 3 in red, and 2 in yellow. I have provided you with enough fabrics to mix and match your arrangement of fabrics for the cross units. As always, I give you permission to be creative with your color choices.

Drunkard's Path Cross Block

1. Sew a single-post unit between 2 Drunkard's Path units, keeping the end piece to the outside edge. Make 18 sets of half-blocks. Press.

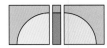

Make 18 half-blocks.

2. Sew a double-post unit between 2 half-blocks, aligning the center seams. Press. Make 9 blocks.

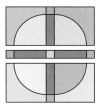

Block assembly—make 9.

Alternate Blocks

1. Fold and press each 8⅞" × 16¾" rectangle in half, right sides together, along the long side.

2. Fold and press each alternate block triangle in half, right sides together, from the point to the center of the long side.

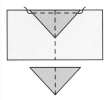

Fold. Fold. Fold.

Fold rectangles and triangles in half.

3. Align the center folds and pin the triangles to the rectangles, right sides together. Sew the triangles to the sides of the rectangles. Press.

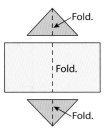

Sew triangles to rectangles.

4. Using the side triangles as corners, cut off the tips of the rectangles to create a 12" × 12" square. Make 4.

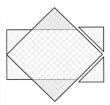

Trim off rectangle tips.

5. Optional: Trace 12 leaves onto the leaf fabric, using the template (page 71). Fuse and topstitch the leaves onto the alternate block using raw-edge or fused-edge appliqué (page 13).

Side Setting Triangles

1. Remove the selvage edges from the 3 strips 5½″ wide and sew them together end to end. Press the seams open.

2. Cut 8 polygon shapes with the long side measuring 17½″. Place the ruler on the fabric and use the 45° mark to create the correct angle (see Tip, page 42).

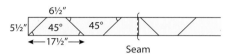

Cut border setting polygons.

3. Fold and press the polygons in half, right sides together, along the long edge and aligning angled edges.

4. Fold and press the setting triangle in half, right sides together, from the point to the center of the long side.

5. Align the center folds, right sides together, and pin the triangle to the short, straight side of the polygon. Sew the triangle to the polygon. Press toward the polygon. (Note: An accurate ¼″ seam allowance is necessary to piece the shapes into a setting triangle.) Trim the triangle tips (page 34). Make 8.

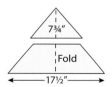

Border setting triangles—make 8.

Quilt Assembly

1. Sew the blocks and side setting triangles together in diagonal rows following the quilt assembly diagram (below). The setting triangles are oversize.

2. Press the rows and trim off the triangle tips that stick out beyond the edges (page 34).

3. Sew the rows together.

4. Press and trim to square up and remove any last triangle points.

5. Sew on the corner triangles, and trim to square up with the edges of the quilt top. Press.

Finishing

Layer, quilt, and bind your quilt (pages 20–21).

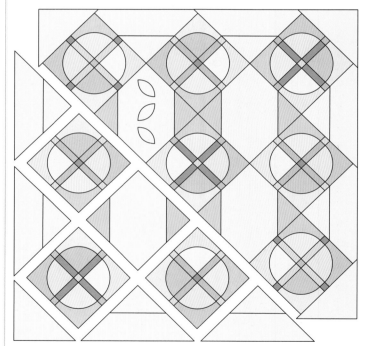

Quilt assembly

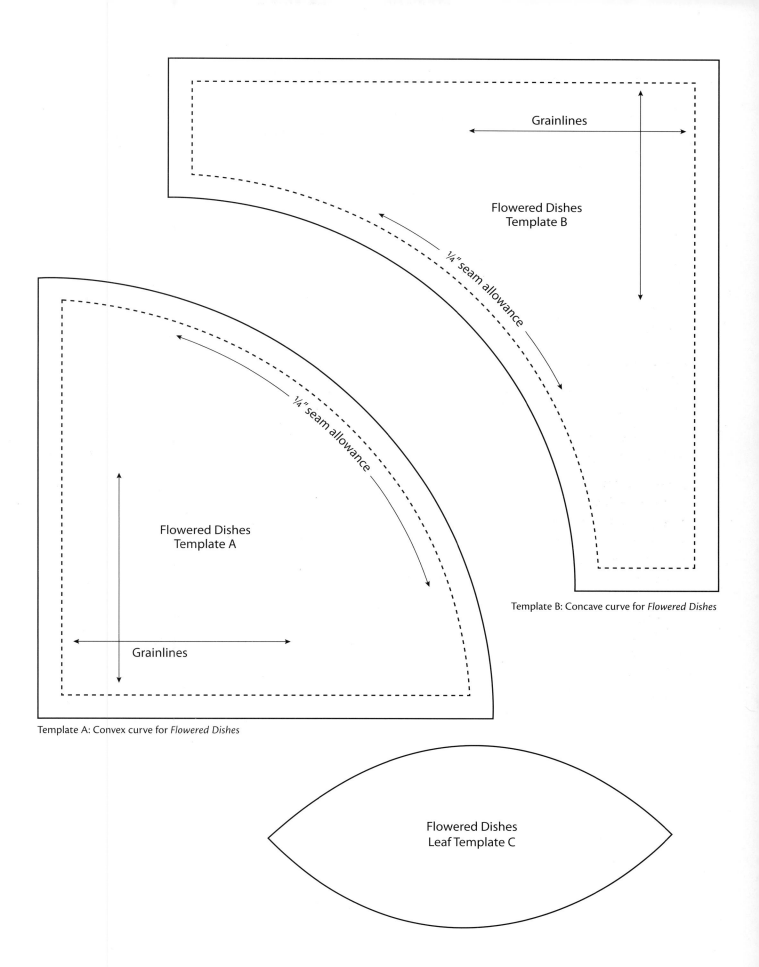

Grainlines

Flowered Dishes
Template B

¼" seam allowance

Flowered Dishes
Template A

¼" seam allowance

Grainlines

Template B: Concave curve for *Flowered Dishes*

Template A: Convex curve for *Flowered Dishes*

Flowered Dishes
Leaf Template C

Asian Dishes, made by Alethea Ballard, machine quilting by Elaine Beatty

Finished quilt: 58½" × 58½"

The large space in the center blocks is a natural spot to showcase some amazing fabric. In this quilt, I used the beautiful women and the gorgeous house to create visual focal points. The luscious blues and rich ombres—fabrics that gradually change color across the width of the yardage—called out to be used. Using ombres created wonderful, subtle color variations. Playing with the floral fabrics and the placement of the matching stems and flowers resulted in a lovely, elegant wall-hanging.

Modern Home Landscape, made by Alethea Ballard

lovely landscape

Fabric panels can be really cool, but when you find one you might not want to cut it into pieces. The layout of *Modern Home Landscape* makes using a large quilt panel fun. An amazing Asian fabric, a funny kids' panel, or a pictorial scene could be used in this quilt design.

Many fabric lines include a large panel as part of the collection, and this gives the quilter a great palette with which to build a quilt. The trick to making this project work is using fabrics that have an interesting pattern, so that they don't read too solid from a distance, and

using fabrics in each of the colors found in the large panel. Try to keep the colors for the circle blocks in the same proportion as they appear in the panel. If there's more blue in the panel than any other color, use more blue. This helps pull the quilt together and gives it an artistic feel.

Each circle block is a delight to make. Provided are three techniques to create the circles, so you can pick your favorite method. After that, the quilt goes together super fast! Whether it is whimsical or elegant, modern or classic, this quilt design can make your large panel look spectacular.

use that fabric: *a panel!*

Use those lovely panels and landscapes! Now you can embrace that large, beautiful pictorial scene and make a delightful wallhanging.

materials

panel or large-scale lengthwise-directional print for quilt center

- ¾ yard

prints #1 for the circles

- ⅔ yard total or 24 pieces 5″ × 5″ in a variety of fabrics

prints #2 for the circle backgrounds

- 1 yard total or 24 pieces 6½″ × 6½″ in a variety of fabrics

note

When selecting fabrics for the circles and circle backgrounds, choose colors found in the quilt center fabric. Use the color spots on the selvage edge for guidance. The same fabrics can be used for both circles and circle backgrounds.

light print for inner border

- ⅜ yard

dark print for outer border

- 1⅛ yards

binding

- ⅝ yard

backing

- 2⅝ yards

batting

- 71″ × 47″

optional notions for circle appliqué

- Gluestick for raw-edge appliqué (page 75)

medium or lightweight fusible web for fused-edge appliqué (page 75)

- 1¼ yards

nonwoven medium or lightweight fusible interfacing for turned-edge appliqué (page 75)

- 1 yard

cutting

panel or large-scale print

- Cut 1 piece 42½″ × 18½″ for the center (see Tip, at right).

prints #1

- Cut 24 squares 5″ × 5″ for the circles.

prints #2

- Cut 24 squares 6½″ × 6½″ for the circle backgrounds.

light print

- Cut 5 strips 1¾″ × width of fabric for the inner border.

dark print

- Cut 6 strips 5½″ × width of fabric for the outer borders.

binding

- Cut 7 strips 2½″ × width of fabric.

tip

If your fabric is too narrow to get a 42½″ wide piece, you can add on to one side using Making Fabric Wider (or Longer), page 9. Or you can just put a little 1″ border on each side. The center just needs to be 42½″ for the circles to fit.

Blocks

Use ¼" seam allowances unless otherwise noted.

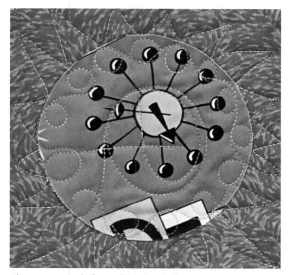

Choose your style for making the circles.

Circle Appliqué

Choose one of the 3 following methods to make the circle blocks:

RAW-EDGE APPLIQUÉ

Use the raw edges as part of the design. Stitch around the circles for a funky look or attach the circles when the quilting is done. See Raw-Edge Appliqué (page 13) for more details.

1. Draw 24 circles using a CD or DVD, or trace the pattern provided (page 77) onto the 5" square fabrics.

2. Cut out circles on the line. Make 24 circles.

3. Apply gluestick to the back of the circles. Center the circles on their corresponding 6½" square background piece. Iron the circles flat to adhere and dry the glue.

FUSED-EDGE APPLIQUÉ

This technique fuses just the edges of the appliqué. You can skip Step 2 and use a whole piece of fusible web. It holds the piece flatter, but can look stiff and is a little thicker for the quilting. Either style is fine.

1. Draw 24 circles using a CD or DVD, or trace the pattern provided (page 77) onto the paper backing of the fusible web.

2. Cut out the circles ¼" *outside* the line. Then trim the circles ¼" inside the line, removing the centers and creating a ring ½" wide.

3. Use the manufacturer's directions to adhere the fusible web to the wrong side of the circle fabric.

4. Cut out the circles on the line. Make 24 circles.

5. Center the circles on their corresponding 6½" square background piece and fuse in place.

TURNED-EDGE APPLIQUÉ

This method takes longer but gives a more structured look and increases the quilt's heirloom quality.

1. Draw 24 circles using a CD or DVD, or trace the pattern provided (page 77) onto the bumpy side of the fusible interfacing. Leave ¾" between the circles.

2. Rough cut the circles apart.

3. Pin the interfacing, bumpy side up, on the right side of a 5" square piece and stitch on the line.

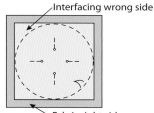

Stitch interfacing to right side of fabric.

4. Trim the interfacing and fabric, leaving a ⅛" seam allowance.

5. Make a straight slit in the center of the interfacing, being careful not to cut through the fabric.

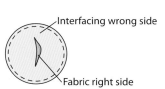

Make slit in interfacing.

6. Gently turn the circle right sides out and use a point turner or your finger to smooth out the curved outer edge.

tip
. . . .

To produce rounder edges on my circles, I always use my fingers to smooth out the curved edges and then press the edges by hand before fusing. Sometimes the interfacing stretches out, but I can fix that when I press.

7. Press the circles flat, fusing the interfacing to the back of the circle fabric. Follow the manufacturer's directions for temperature and pressing time.

8. Center the circles on the 6½" squares and pin them in place. Topstitch or hand appliqué the circles to the squares.

Quilt Assembly

1. Sew 3 circle blocks together and attach them to one of the 18½" sides of the center fabric. Press. Repeat for the other side.

2. Sew 9 circle blocks together and attach them to the top of the center fabric. Press. Repeat for the bottom.

Borders

For more detailed information about adding borders, see Measure, Pin, and Sew, page 19.

tip
. . . .

I added a little yellow accent in the blue inner border to break up the visual line and add interest. To do this, cut your border fabric into random-sized sections and sew accent squares or triangles between them.

Inner Border

1. Measure vertically through the center of the quilt top and trim the 2 side inner borders to this length.

2. Sew the side inner borders to the quilt top. Press.

3. Trim off the selvage edges of the remaining 3 strips and, using a small stitch length, join them into 1 long strip. Press the seams open.

4. Measure horizontally through the center of the quilt top and cut 2 strips to that length.

5. Sew the top and bottom inner borders to the quilt top. Press.

Outer Border

1. Cut 2 pieces 1¾" × 5½" from the leftover inner border strips.

2. Trim off the selvage edges of one of the 5½" outer border strips. Sew a 1¾" × 5½" inner border piece to the bottom edge of the strip, creating the right-side outer border.

3. Repeat Step 2, sewing the 1¾" × 5½" inner border piece to the top edge of an outer border strip, creating the left outer border.

4. Measure vertically through the center of the quilt top and trim the side borders to that length, being sure not to trim off the extra 1¾" strip that was added.

5. Sew the side outer borders to the corresponding edges of the quilt top, aligning the pieced seams. Press.

6. Trim off the selvage edges of the remaining 4 strips. Join 2 of the strips into 1 long strip, using a small stitch length. Repeat with the remaining 2 strips. Press the seams open.

7. Measure horizontally through the center of the quilt top and trim the 2 strips to this length.

8. Sew the top and bottom borders to the quilt top. Press and trim to square up, if necessary.

Maverick Quilter Says
Why stop with just one panel? Make more circles and use more panels like I did in the *Geisha Landscape* quilt (page 78). Making the borders funky, patched, or wonky can work too. It is so fun to let the fabric guide you into making new creative choices and working in new ways.

Finishing

Layer, quilt, and bind your quilt (pages 20–21).

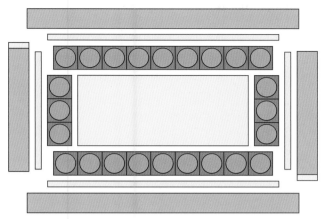

Quilt assembly

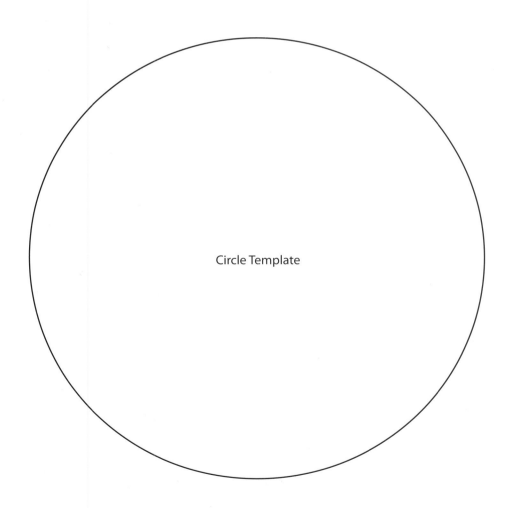

Circle Template

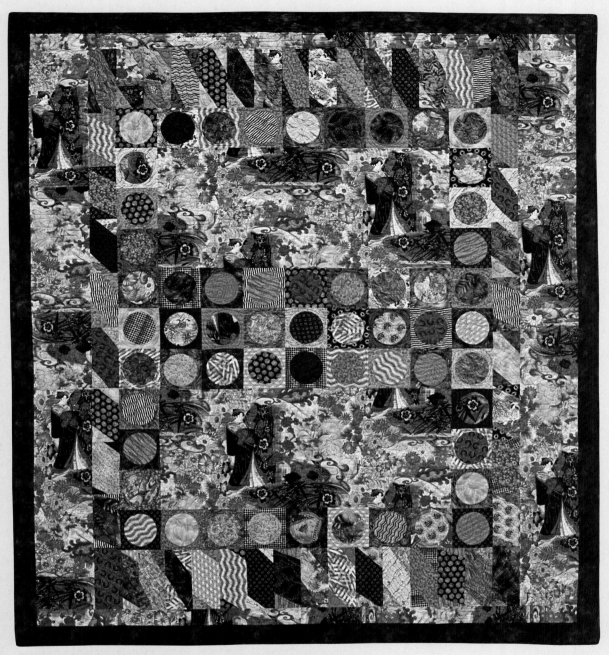

Geisha Landscape, made by Alethea Ballard, machine quilting by Laura Lee Fritz

Finished quilt: 82" × 91"

This quilt was made as a wedding gift for two of my oldest and dearest friends. They are both artistic, and I wanted something very special and unique for them. In retrospect, I see that this was the first quilt where I chose the fabric first and let the quilt design reveal itself as I worked. It was also the first time I chose individual fabrics simply for their colors and varied patterns, rather than fabrics that were cute or pretty. I jazzed things up with the pieced borders, which helped enlarge it to a bed-size quilt. This was an important turning point in my work. Sometimes working out of your comfort zone yields the best results!

about the author

Photo by Stephen Whiteside

Alethea Ballard gets very excited about fabric and quilts. Just bring up the subject, and she is off and running. Unable to stop the creative ideas from flowing, she likes to make just about everything it is possible to make using fabric: from household items to bags, from appliqué quilts to dolls and pillowcases for charity. Living in the San Francisco Bay Area is paradise for Alethea because she has a dozen amazing fabric sources within her reach. And, of course, there's always the Internet if that's not enough.

Mostly self-taught, Alethea has tried just about every kind of quilt technique and, over the years, has focused her attention on bright, large-scale, and conversation fabrics and how to transform them into fresh and interesting quilts. Buying fabric she likes when she sees it ensures that she always has inspiration and a fabulous palette to work from when the whimsy of a new idea strikes her.

Alethea's working style is a culmination of her impatience with convention, her impulsiveness, and her artistic sensibility. She prefers to work quickly and spontaneously, using simple images and playing with the clear, bright colors she loves.

As both a quilt teacher and middle school home economics teacher, Alethea loves to convey her ideas, artistic visions, and passions to a variety of ages and skill levels.

With the recent purchase of a longarm quilting machine, she began to design and create quilts that were bigger, bolder, and quirkier than ever before. Now she finds herself ready to bust out and be a true quilt maverick.

Alethea invites you to join her for the fun that maverick quilting can be!

Alethea Ballard is on the World Wide Web at Maverickquilts.com.

Also by Alethea Ballard:

Great Titles *from* C&T PUBLISHING

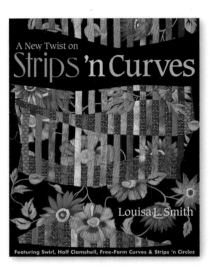

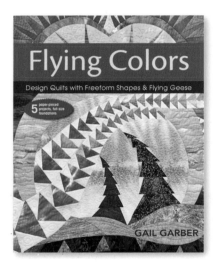

Available at your local retailer or **www.ctpub.com** *or* **800-284-1114**